the **committee**

TAD & ALYSHA,
GOOD TO SEE YOU GUYS,
GOD HAS AN AWESOME CALL
ON YOU GUYS. ENJOY
THE BOOK!
GOD BLESS,

the **committee**

they **decide** if i live or die...

a true story by ***clay cornelius***

TATE PUBLISHING *&* *Enterprises*

Published by Tate Publishing & Enterprises, LLC

127 E. Trade Center Terrace | Mustang, Oklahoma 73064 USA

1.888.361.9473 | www.tatepublishing.com

Tate Publishing is committed to excellence in the publishing industry. The company reflects the philosophy established by the founders, based on Psalms 68:11,
"The Lord gave the word and great was the company of those who published it."

Book design copyright © 2007 by Tate Publishing, LLC. All rights reserved.
Cover design by Lynly D. Taylor
Interior design by Elizabeth A. Mason

Published in the United States of America

ISBN: 978-1-6024781-0-7

1. Adult, Non-fiction 2. Christian

3. Substance Abuse

07.07.03

table of contents

chapter 1: **christmas 2001**

My typical American family celebrates Christmas the same way every year. The agenda is engrained in our minds, and programmed after years of repetition. My two younger sisters and I meet up at my mom's house, arriving from wherever each of us happens to be living that year. My mom has the Christmas music on hand and playing non-stop; she has been listening to it in anticipation since before Thanksgiving. The evening of Christmas Eve, I put in my yearly token hour of church with the family, and afterward my mom pesters us until we agree to drive around town for a few minutes to look at the Christmas lights. Then we head home for the night, nursing our dwindling anticipation for the next morning.

Christmas Day we all get up and pretend we're kids again for a few minutes. Not surprisingly, "Santa" has visited our house, filled our stockings, and left gifts strewn about. We excitedly open our presents and the stockings my mom refuses to eliminate despite our age. We eat Christmas brunch, and then we head to my dad's house where a second gift opening commences with our step-family. Throughout Christmas Day are various visits to grandparents and relatives, with the apparent objective of collecting gifts, money, and snacks. Finally, late in the evening, Christmas dinner is served, and we end up going to bed fatter and wealthier than when we woke up. Sure, each Christmas offers a few schedule shifts and variances, but our agenda remains similar every year.

Christmas of 2001 was no exception. After I graduated from college in May, I returned to my small Northern Michigan hometown of Alpena to begin my "adult life." Once there, I was re-hired to the professional-level, number-crunching job at which I had interned over the previous summer. The five minute drive from my apartment to my mom's house on Christmas Eve was no problem for me. My middle sister was in her junior year of college downstate, and had made the lengthy drive home days earlier, after finals week was over. My youngest sister was a senior in high school, and still had about a year left under my mom's roof. Both my sisters were at my mom's when I got there.

As I walked in the door at about six in the evening, my mom's familiar Christmas tunes met me. Mom's CD collection was expansive; her Christmas CDs were usually the same songs, sung by whoever happened to be popular that year. I thought I recognized that year's "featured artist" as Mariah Carey.

Of course, everybody was happy to see each other, or at least we acted that way. I loved my family, but now that I was back in town, my friends had taken a more predominant role in my life, and I kind of wanted to be with them. But one thing I was always happy to see at my mom's house was the food, and we sat around the living room snacking and chatting before piling into her van and heading off to church.

My mom had always been a strong advocate of church attendance. Beginning around age thirteen, I began to put up some resistance toward going to church, especially after being forced into those dull catechism classes. Now, as my independence blossomed at age twenty-two, neither my mother's Lutheran church that had been in the family for generations, nor my father's eccentric backwoods church, ever got the satisfaction of my attendance. After all, I was an adult; I could do what I wanted. I knew, however, that avoiding the traditional Christmas and Easter services would create way too much of a fuss, so I consented on those two days per year.

There I sat in church on Christmas Eve, in the balcony, as I had so many Christmases before. The Lutherans took their religion very mechanically, with nearly every word or song repeated directly out of the bulletin or hymnal. The only moments that offered any spontaneity were during the upcoming twelve-minute sermon. I sat in the pew sarcastically asking myself what the Pastor was going to preach about this year. I knew it was going to be something to do with the manger scene that adorned the altar, just like every year before. I wondered if the topic would be Mary, Joseph, or maybe the Wise Men this year, but I didn't care. By the time he got around to giving the lesson, I was already thinking about girls or gifts or money, whatever thoughts cascaded through my mind to alleviate the boredom. I had heard "the Christmas story" a hundred times before, and at that point in my life, it was about as real to me as Santa Claus.

Finally, the service was over, and we got back into the van. My sisters and I knew exactly what was coming, as my mom tried to subtly comment on how "nice it would be" to drive around and look at the Christmas lights. A short debate ensued, as was tradition, and we made some sort of agreement to pacify my mom, much like we did with church. We drove around and saw *some* of the lit-up houses, but not *all* of them, per our negotiation. Then we headed home for the night.

It was at this time that I decided a slight departure from tradition was in order. The idea had entered my mind while I was resisting the doldrums of church. In light of my recently acquired independence, I decided I was going to celebrate the late hours of Christmas Eve with my friends, and spend the night at my apartment instead of my mom's house. I had put in my shift with the family, and it was time to cut loose for a little while.

Of course this tradition-breaking idea was met with immediate resistance from a predictable source—my mother. "Just spend one night with us," she pleaded. "We can play board games," she said, failing to entice me. Surprisingly, my sisters also seemed to be on her side. Usually they vindicated my independence, since both of them were also approaching new levels of it. But tonight, my mother and sisters repeatedly asked me to stay at home for "just one night." But my mind was made up.

"I'll be back tomorrow morning by nine o'clock," I assured them as I headed out the door.

I hopped in my car, considering that night's plans. I was driving a Plymouth Colt Vista, a beautiful medley of a small car mixed with van. In other words, it was not a very "hip" ride. I had bought it from my grandma at a price I couldn't refuse, with the only drawback being the inherent uncoolness. But it was a dependable car. I shut the door and quickly dialed my best friend on my bulky cell phone. He thought a little Christmas celebration would be great, so I told him I would pick him up from his mom's after I swung by the party store for a little beer.

I headed to the liquor store closest to my mom's house, but as I was approaching, I noticed the sign was not lit up. I pulled into the parking lot of the run-down store, and indeed it had closed a little while earlier that evening. I was surprised, but not defeated by any means. There were plenty of party stores in town.

I soon found out that although there were plenty of stores, not one of them was open or would sell alcohol late Christmas Eve night. Each store I tried left me a little more annoyed at this predicament. Annoyance became frustration, and frustration became anger. *What is wrong with these places?* I asked myself. *I'm a valued customer! They're missing out on good business!* I ranted for a few minutes, and then began to focus on the problem that had left me so upset. Where was I going to get some beer?

I pulled into my buddy's mom's driveway and sat there for a minute, regaining my composure. *This anger was a little unexpected, but justified under these circumstances, right?* I asked myself. I really didn't have time to wonder long before my friend jumped in the car with me. Keeping the majority of my anger in check, I shared my frustration with my friend as we headed to my apartment. He too wanted a few beers, so we put our heads together and tried to think of somewhere we could get some. *At least we have a temporary solution in my apartment,* I thought as we pulled into my driveway.

We entered my place as we had so many times before, greeted by the ever-growing clutter-piles. My single-bedroom apartment was small and poorly furnished, mainly with odds and ends my friends and family had been discarding. The living and dining area was fast-becoming a virtual garbage dump. Strewn everywhere were malt liquor forty bottles, mostly ultra-cheap "Big Bear" brand; remnants of parties past. There literally had to be at least a hundred of them. Dispersed among them were McDonald's and other fast food wrappers, discarded bags of chips and candy, and a fine variety of empty wine and liquor bottles. The bedroom was dedicated to clothes piles, and the tiny bathroom was growing unsanitary. I just really hated cleaning, on account of the fact that it cut into my "having fun."

We assumed our usual positions. I sat down in my favorite chair, and he sat on my dilapidated couch, both facing the TV. I opened the small compartment door of the lamp stand next to my chair, and pulled out a small plastic bag filled with the buds of a green plant we affectionately referred to as "pot."

I was a big fan of rolling the pot up in a cigar wrapper, called a "blunt," while my friend was more into pipes and bongs. So if I had the bag, we were rolling blunts, and if he had the bag, it was pipe time. Usually both of us had a bag, so splitting a joint was a good compromise, although it wasn't like we only smoked once a night. We started our Christmas celebration that year with a blunt, and we sat there staring at the TV for a few minutes before we remembered our dilemma.

The pot helped me to chill out a little more regarding the alcohol issue, but solving the problem and finding some beer was still priority one. We started to call various friends, acquaintances, even coworkers, looking for beer, and willing to pay any price. As sobriety loomed in our immediate futures, my best friend stumbled across one of his coworkers who had some extra cases of beer, and was actually feeling lonely that Christmas. She had put her kids to bed and was sitting up watching TV, so we excitedly headed over to her apartment to continue our Christmas celebration.

Once I got that first beer to my lips, I could finally relax again. We sat around her kitchen table talking and playing cards, smoking cigarettes, or whatever. The events were insignificant to me; I had my alcohol. Finally the search was over and I thought that my night was complete. The rest was cruise control; get drunk, smoke some weed, and then get drunker and smoke some more.

But somewhere between drunk and drunker, things started to go awry again. This time it was not an exterior event that created the conflict, but instead something inside of me. My friend and his coworker were chatting away, but I was sitting there deep in thought. Everything seemed to be in proper place; I had my much-sought-after buzz, with the assurance of as much drinking and smoking as I could want for the night. But something was still wrong. I started to wonder why I had gotten so upset about the simple prospect of spending Christmas Eve sober. My question from earlier returned, and I began to wonder if such anger was truly justifiable.

As I reflected on this, I made a startling discovery. Turning away from my family to go drinking on Christmas Eve should have given me a clue. The countless bottles in my apartment should have tipped me off. But I had proceeded with ignorance until that Christmas Eve. In college, I had learned to juggle partying and school decently, but I admittedly could not have completed another semester at the rate I was going. Upon my return to Alpena six months prior, I had bumped the stakes up to the next level as I started to incorporate a career into my juggling act. That Christmas Eve night, in my friend's coworker's apartment, I realized that I had been getting drunk and smoking pot every single night since my return to town.

The anger I had felt earlier that night raised a red flag for me. It told me that something was wrong with my priorities. Of course, I didn't want to accept this easily, so I quickly came up with a little justification. *I don't need to party to have fun,* I uncertainly reassured myself. I didn't feel any better.

Something inside me made a lasting impression on my life that night, but I didn't like it. Something told me my life was going in the wrong direction. I tried not to listen, but it kept picking at me, pestering me. Maybe it had tried to get my attention before, and I had drowned it in alcohol or pot, but that Christmas Eve was the first night I heard it clearly. My options for the evening were either to quit partying and go home for the night, or to try to drown that pestering voice again. I opted to drown it.

That night, I got rip-roaring drunk and high as a kite, and I shut that voice out. Past that point, the details get a little hazy. Later on, I drove my friend home, drunk of course, and made it to my apartment to crash out for the night, thinking that I had succeeded in eliminating the voice that told me something was wrong with my life. I was mistaken.

date: december 25, 2001
purpose: year-end review
agenda: status reports, upcoming-year
          planning

The Committee sat around the oval table in the dimly lit boardroom, with the drab, gray, windowless walls surrounding them. The chairman came in and sat in his seat, wearing a wrinkled black suit and tie that looked like it had been pulled out of a hamper and thrown on in less than two minutes. He called the meeting to order.

"I'm really sorry about this, guys," he began. "But you know how it works. From time to time we've got to have these silly status updates, and year-end happens to be that time. I know it's kind of a speed-bump in the festivities, but all we have to do is agree that everything is great, and we can get out of here in five minutes. As far as I can see, everything *is* great, so I don't foresee any problems or issues arising. We can just say this year was good, and continue doing the same things we did this year into the next year. Sound good, everyone?" He didn't wait for a response, and began to stand up. "Okay, great, meeting adjourned, see you all at the six-month..."

"Hold on a second," interrupted one of the members.

"Yes?" asked the chairman politely.

An older man stood to his feet. He looked to be around fifty, clean-cut and humble-looking. His light brown hair was parted on the side and about half-way-through age's whitening process. He wore a white collared shirt and a solid-blue tie that almost matched his black dress pants. "Something's not right here," he stammered, with a slight hint of a Southern accent. "I don't know what it is, and I know some of you feel it too, but all I can tell is that something's not right."

The rest of the Committee members turned silently toward the chairman, awaiting his response.

"Good to see you, my friend," responded the chairman. "It's been a while, hasn't it? All we need you to do is sit on down, and we can be done with this boring meeting. Okay? Thanks."

But the man didn't sit down. "I'm not going to sit down 'til you hear me. Somethin' just isn't right."

"Is it your wardrobe?" asked the chairman sarcastically, trying to play off this disruption. Grinning, he looked around the boardroom for approval. Getting little, he turned back to business. "What exactly do you mean? What particularly isn't right?"

"Don't know," the man answered, undaunted by the insult, "but I know it's somethin'."

"We really need a little more to go on than that," said the chairman. "How are we going to correct 'something'?"

"I can't tell," replied the man. "I'm just sayin' something's wrong. That's what I do, I say if something's wrong. And something's wrong."

"Okay, okay, how about this, buddy?" asked the chairman, becoming more agitated at the seemingly pointless delay. "Everybody, I have an announcement. Please keep an eye out for 'something' being wrong, and we'll discuss 'something' at the six-month status-report meeting. Now, if there are no more items of business, we can wrap this one up. Have a great Christmas, guys."

With that, the chairman stood up and tried to inconspicuously rush out the door, apparently for another engagement. The older man and the rest of the members filtered out slowly, looking over reports or chatting, as a typical business meeting ends. But one member, the very first member appointed, stayed in his seat, contemplating the somewhat bizarre and unspecific warning of the older man.

chapter 2: **infancy**

Christmas morning, I didn't wake up to a tree surrounded by presents like I had every Christmas before. I instead woke up to the after-effects of a night of drinking, like I had every day for the past six months. That Christmas morning, my hangover seemed to be particularly noticeable. I dragged myself out of bed to make my nine o'clock deadline at my mom's house. I jumped into my Colt Vista, still half-asleep and half-drunk, and sped over.

Once I arrived at my mom's, Christmas could get underway. "Family time" was not my favorite activity, especially at 9:00 a.m. with a hangover. But the pay-off was the presents. My mom always went all-out to make sure her kids got showered with gifts on Christmas. It was almost like a bribe for our continued visitations. And though she could buy my physical presence, my polluted mind was still my own. As I quickly became bored with family bonding, my thoughts began to roam. For some reason, I wasn't thinking about the usual girls, drinks, and drugs that my favorite lyrics glorified. Sitting with my sisters and mother in the living room, I actually spent a few minutes thinking about my life and my family.

I knew I was in a room with three other people, but it felt like there were others. Some of my relatives celebrated Christmas elsewhere. Some of my grandparents had passed on. But there in that living room were many of the smiling faces I had known and loved, staring back at me through the frozen eyes of their photographs. On the walls and shelves throughout my mother's house were pictures of some of the most influential people in my life—my roots. And though I was bored, I couldn't help but smile to think of all they had contributed to my upbringing.

There was a picture of my great-grandparents, whom I had the honor of knowing. I could still remember my great-grandpa's humble prayers at our family get-togethers. I'm pretty sure his favorite cologne was Ben Gay. There was a picture of my grandpa, with his subtle tips that went a short way toward improving my golf game or my attitude. He had been a definite role model in my life following my parents' divorce, but had unfortunately passed on before I was "fully developed." Maybe I should have listened better while he was around. There were other pictures of my parents, often beaming with pride in their children. Aunts and uncles, family friends, and other relatives had all made a noticeable contribution to the man I had become. Each of my elders had in some way made an impact on my life, with none more influential than my mom and dad.

Of course, I loved my parents, and of course I thought they were squares. They were the original "government" that my partying was rebelling against. Growing up, my mom had always taught me to "do the right thing." She instituted such practical guidelines as bedtimes, curfews, and mandatory events, which included many seeming unpleasantries such as church, the dentist, the doctor, and visiting family. All of that discipline in my life was of course for my benefit, but that didn't make it any more exciting to a child. She taught me to stay away from troublemakers in school and to obey the teachers and authority figures. She always chose the safe, conservative path through life.

Many of her teachings were effectively instilled in my adult life, but some were not. Of course she opposed things like getting drunk or doing drugs. She was forever trying to make me promise I wouldn't drink and drive—a promise I couldn't make. I rebelled directly against her standards, with my college and post-college behavior being the pinnacle of such disregard. But that didn't mean the things she had told me were completely forgotten. I could still remember most of her lessons; I was just too busy forging my own path to worry about them.

My dad also had his share of impact on my life, though his lessons were typically church-related. He was a strong disciplinarian, but when my parents got divorced, he lost some of his ability to influence my life. Still, he wouldn't hesitate to break out that big boring Bible that made us kids sigh impatiently. He taught us morals similar to my mom's—that we needed to always choose "the right thing" when presented with an option. His views were often more general and hard-to-grasp than the practical teachings of my mom. Regardless, both parents played a significant role in helping me to determine what was right and what was wrong.

I knew my parents loved me, so even though I didn't always obey, I tried to listen. I tried to at least give them that respect, even though, practically speaking, their ramblings often went in one ear and out the other. But my parents weren't the only people who had influenced me. My life had a cavalcade of these "positive" influences, from family to school to church. I didn't always obey, but I listened, even if it was sometimes only subconsciously.

I loved all of my family members and had a unique relationship with each one of them. I would like to have said that I loved them all equally, but I had a favorite. He appeared in a number of the photos around my mother's home. I would *always* listen to him no matter what others said. At that stage in my life, *I* was my favorite family member. That's why I left my mom's the night before—because *I* wanted to. That's why I drank and smoked pot. I was so smart, nobody could tell me anything. I spent a lot of my time thinking about me and doing things for me.

I began on June 2, 1979. My birth was the beginning of the life I had come to be so proud of. And though that June 2nd was a pretty important day for my existence, I didn't remember one minute of it. Fortunately, the two most significant influences in my life, my mom and dad, had been very willing to fill me in on the details. I was my parents' first child, so it was new territory for both of them. And, of course, me. Nobody knew exactly what to expect. The pregnancy seemed to be going normally, until it was time for me to be born and I didn't want to emerge from my cozy nine-month incubation chamber. The situation became critical, as I was not making the necessary moves to be born naturally. The environment that had kept me alive for the past three trimesters was fast becoming a suffocating death-chamber. Eventually, the doctors were forced to operate, performing a cesarean-section that saved me and gave me my first breath.

I made it through the surgery, or did *I*? At my birth, I obviously had very limited ability to process data. So in retrospect, I had to consider how much *I* really had to do with my survival. I was undeniably alive, but I had to ask myself *Why did I pull through?* I wondered how much *I* actually had to do with it.

Undoubtedly, my instinct as an unborn child was to live. I essentially had two options in that critical situation of my birth. Choice number one was to live, which seemed to be the natural choice. Choice number two was the alternative to living, which was probably the easy choice. And somehow, the decision was made that I would live. I didn't know what made that decision for me; maybe chance, maybe survival instinct. But no reasoning or analysis was going to get me through that life-or-death situation. Regardless of what chose "life" for me, all I could do as baby was to hang on to that decision.

I did hang on, and it proved to be a worthwhile choice. The world was a magical place of wonder for a baby. Once I got through the whole birthing-and-hospital process, I began to explore the world around me as I entered a new phase of my life. I no longer had to fight for my survival, and instead could begin to process what was going on around me. My parents gave me tons of love, as did most every stranger that I came in contact with. Everyone, especially those I would come to know as family, was willing to make funny faces and sounds to amuse me. And most of them succeeded in amusing me, but it wasn't a difficult task. *Anything* made me happy. "Happy" was my default setting. I didn't need control of my life; my parents took care of that. I didn't need the latest toy or trinket; any brightly colored object would do. All I needed was existence in order to be happy.

Sure, as a baby I had sad moments, like when a full diaper or an empty stomach robbed me of my comfort. But happiness was only a change or a meal away. It never seemed to feel distant like it sometimes had during "adult life." As a baby, my existence was guaranteed and so was my happiness, as far as I knew.

As I grew, I developed my basic mental and motor skills, which gave me more ability to explore my environment. Of course, my environment was usually a crib or a playpen, so there was only so much to explore. But I still had plenty to keep me amused. When my two-year-old brain was trying to plan the agenda for the next thirty seconds, the goal was clear: Find something that makes me happy. Stare at this, play with that, stick this in my mouth. I often wished my adult agenda was still that simple. In fact, I wished I was still that happy. But I decided that the lack of happiness was the price of my "incredible wisdom," and that my diminishing levels of joy were because I knew too much about the "real world" to be so ignorantly blissful.

As my world was growing beyond the playpen, my parents decided it was time for a change. My first sister had been born, so when I was three we moved from our small house into a much larger log cabin my dad had been building. We called this new house the "woods house" because it was about a half-mile down a two-track road back in the woods. This huge house gave me a seemingly infinite amount of play space, and tons of new areas to explore. For days and weeks and months, I wandered around the huge stone fireplace, through the bedrooms, and into the kitchen. It was in the kitchen that I made an interesting discovery one day.

I had heard the word "hot" on many occasions before. I knew what it meant. And when my parents told me the stove was hot, and not to touch it, I listened and understood. But once I was left unsupervised for just a few minutes, I decided to try something naughty in the interest of environment-exploration. I reached out my tiny, curious hand and touched the door on our old wood stove.

In that moment, I realized that the book definition of the word "hot" was a whole lot different than the actual meaning. My first reaction to the pain was of course crying. But more important than my initial despair was the fact that I learned never to touch the hot stove again. I also learned that maybe my mommy and daddy knew a thing or two about life and its dangers. But no lecture they could have given would have taught me any better than actually subjecting myself to that ignorance-induced pain. I could never understand the value of obedience until I got a first-hand look at the consequence of disobedience. All I knew was that I didn't ever want to feel that pain again, and wouldn't, if I could help it. That pain had taught me a valuable lesson.

Pain continued in those early days to teach me that I did not want to mess with it. My parents often used pain to penalize me if I misbehaved, in the form of a nice, healthy spanking. And no message came in more loud and clear than physical pain. I eventually made the necessary connections to realize that if I disobeyed, I got spanked. And somehow, those two parental units were too smart to outwit with my primitive deception tactics. The simple solution was to quit disobeying. So I tried to be obedient, listening respectfully to their instruction. Most of the time, it made sense. And I knew there were plenty of fun things I could do that were not naughty, such as playing with my toys, so I tried to stick to them.

By the time I was four, I had amassed a small collection of trinkets and toys. I played with them all, but my favorite was Lego blocks. I had recently graduated from the jumbo-sized "camper blocks" to the much smaller, more-intricate, interlocking Legos. I played with them for hours, creatively constructing cars and planes and houses, only to rip them apart and rebuild. I rarely followed the directions in the boxes; I was too busy coming up with my own ideas. My projects had to meet two criteria; they had to look good and they had to utilize moving pieces properly, like doors, hinges, and wheels. I loved to expand my mind by developing new creations.

My creativity and analytical abilities had begun their development then, and had served me well over the years. Eighteen years later, I had a good job, and a large part of that job was based on my ability to construct visually appealing and fully functional computer spreadsheets. My computer ability was somehow linked to those Legos I started with so many years before, much like the way I was somehow linked to all of the experiences of my past. That clever four-year-old child was still a small part of me, and a small part of who I would become.

profile: conscience

To me, the classic depiction of my conscience was a little angel sitting on my shoulder, giving input as I faced life's challenges. And of course, opposite that little angel on the other shoulder was my "anti-conscience," fittingly depicted in the form of a little devil. The angel-type character was the side of good, telling me that I shouldn't flip that other driver off or steal a coworker's donut. And of course the devil sat there telling me that both these ideas were great. That devil was always coming up with some scheme to get me in trouble, and under the classic depiction, it was all the angel could do to try to convince me otherwise.

The classic conscience was a good representation, but life was a lot more complicated for me than two little voices. Decisions didn't seem to always be a matter of "right" and "wrong." There was a lot of gray area most of the time. It usually seemed like there were hundreds or thousands of little factors that played a role in how my mind analyzed the options in life. In other words, that Christmas Eve, there was a lot more than just one little devil whispering in my ear that I should get all drunked-up. Physical, mental, and social factors all played a role in my decision to binge. Each area contributed its own special addition backing my alcohol and drug abuse. My body wanted "ultimate relaxation," beyond what was possible by just kicking back in a recliner. My mind wanted to forget about the troubles of life for a little while. My friends said it was cool to "party it up," and just have a good time. So there were at least three "devils" whispering in my ear, and I listened to them all, and obeyed. I thought I couldn't go wrong with democracy.

Contrary to the classic conscience depiction, the little entities telling me that it was acceptable to get plastered weren't sitting on my shoulders. Realistically, it was more like they met in a special place I had set aside for them in the back of my mind, which I visualized as a conference room. And they weren't little devils or angels; they were human beings, adequately suited in appearance to represent the influences that made an impact on my decision making. Who in their right mind would listen to a red demon or a guy in a white dress with wings? When I came across a dilemma or a dispute, I would call on these specially-tailored influences to meet together in that room and arrive at a conclusion.

Many little factors tried to influence the decisions I needed to make, and it was my responsibility to weed out the riff-raff. A lot of insignificant factors had tried to worm their way into this boardroom, but I was a strict gatekeeper. I would only allow the influences I knew were important. By age twenty-two, I had narrowed this group down to nine members who, combined, comprised ninety-nine percent of the influences in my life. These nine characters would meet together at my request to choose a path through indecision.

That Christmas Eve, this "committee" had not met in a while, and why should they? What decision or dilemma was I facing? My life was going great as far as I was concerned; I had a job, an apartment, and an increasing circle of friends. I really had nothing I had to solve or correct, as far as I knew. But one member had disagreed. One member had stood to his feet and boldly stated that something was wrong. That member's name was "Conscience."

Conscience was the embodiment of my loved ones' teachings in my life. He was the bits and pieces of advice I had retained over the years from my parents and others close to me. He was the part of me that essentially told me what was right and what was wrong, often by standards above my own. Conscience had lost a lot of pull with the Committee as I began to pursue my *own* goals, not the ones my parents had laid out for me. Determining what was "right" and "wrong" in my life had been effectively delegated to the other members of the Committee. I really didn't enjoy listening to anyone telling me I was wrong and, as a result, nobody in the Committee paid much attention to Conscience. Eventually, the shift began to bother him.

Conscience wasn't the smartest member, and he was usually just a silent observer at meetings. He tried to dress properly with his shirt and tie, but really didn't have much idea about fashion or style. He was a nice older man, but often came across to the other members as clueless when it came to how "reality" worked. Still, from time to time, he would chime in, and out of respect, the other members would at least let him share his viewpoint before they decided against it. That year's Christmas meeting was no exception, as the other members had patronized him through his complaining, thinking nothing of it. *Most* of the other members. But this time, Conscience might have been on to something.

profile: life

Life was the first-appointed member to the Committee. He was about thirty, with short brown hair and a well-trimmed goatee and mustache. His clothes were fairly casual—usually a patterned button-down shirt and khakis. He was a very nice guy, and had a quiet, confident air about him. Like Conscience, he remained silent most of the time, waiting for others to ask his opinion. This happened rarely.

Life became a part of the Committee during the critical moments of my birth. As I was approaching death before I was born, I had a decision to make. Sure, the doctors were in a mad scramble playing their part, but the choice before me was "life" or "death." How could I ever make that decision on my own as an infant? I really couldn't, but Life jumped in and made that decision for me, and I clung to Life through the struggle. Life said, "Survive!" so I survived.

Every human is born with Life—the desire to live and survive—though it often diminishes over the years. Life assured me that my existence, the journey that followed my birth, would be worth the struggle. He continued to offer such assurance, and I naturally put him in charge of my decisions—the beginning of the Committee. In those early hours of my life, what did I have to think about, except survival? Preserving Life was my only priority.

Some call birth "the gift of life," and it might as well have been. I didn't know where it came from, but I didn't want to lose it. I knew from the start that Life was a good thing, healthy for me. And on the day of my birth, Life was in full glory. Through the blood and the mess, through the pain and the suffering, Life was a beautiful thing. Life was the only thing.

In more recent times, however, Life's influence had been on a constant decline as more members were allowed into the Committee. Shortly after my birth, I didn't have to fight for my survival anymore, so even though I owed Life my existence, he was eventually demoted. I continued to take his presence for granted, and my desires for pleasure and money became more prominent. I assumed that Life would always be there. From time to time, a near-death experience or a provocative movie might have made me think about his importance, but for the most part, his role on the Committee had become honorary. I eventually requested that Life just fade into the background so the more important members could discuss the *real* issues in my life.

And Life fell into that background role quite well. He was a deep thinker and planner, no doubt about that. He very rarely would contribute to the Committee anymore unless he was asked to specifically. He just sat there at the table, always in deep thought. And that's exactly what he was doing that Christmas after the meeting—sitting alone in that boardroom, thinking and planning. Conscience had struck a chord with him.

profile: happiness

Happiness was the second member added to the Committee. He was an eight-year-old boy, who always wore the same yellow and orange striped T-shirt and jean shorts. His thick blonde hair was styled in the classic bowl-cut. He was another reserved member like Life and Conscience, typically abiding by the "don't-speak-unless-spoken-to" rule. His age did not command much respect from the other members.

At birth, I had two options: life or death. Once Life was in place, new options began to present themselves, and I began to assemble the Committee in a way that took these new options into consideration. Shortly after choosing Life, I encountered a new choice; I could either feel happy or sad. Under the guidance of Life, I made the logical decision to choose Happiness whenever possible. So Happiness became the second member of my Committee.

When my two-year-old brain was deciding what to do for the day, Happiness would direct my path. Life could relax while I explored my options for creating joy. Blocks made me happy, so I played with them for a while. Then I switched over to stuffed animals, and then to my toy cars. The decisions were easy, since almost everything I came in contact with gave me some amount of happiness. I knew even then that I wanted Happiness around for my entire life. I was so filled with Happiness.

As I recounted the years of my life, it seemed that Happiness had been on a steady decline since my youth. Happiness, like Life, had taken a serious demotion on the Committee when it was decided that other matters were "more-pressing." As a child, Happiness was natural. But as an adult, it required some work. Those seven building blocks I had as a child no longer mesmerized me; I had to seek higher stimuli. And seeking took work, and work was not pleasurable. And because pleasure ruled my life, I indirectly wasn't maintaining Happiness.

I didn't understand much about Happiness, but all I really knew was that I wasn't happy anymore. And apparently I didn't know how to get happy either. None of my selfish techniques were working at all. It was Conscience who presented the idea that a problem might exist in my life, but it was the absence of Happiness that actually verified that problem. Because Happiness was diminishing daily, something had to change.

profile: pleasure

Pleasure was the third member appointed to the Committee. He was a good-looking man of about twenty-five. He usually wore a suit and tie, though it was strictly out of duty that he "dressed up" and combed his hair. He was outgoing and likeable, but a little arrogant as well. He had always been cynical about the meeting process, as it usually stood in the way of his goals. Still, he knew he had to attend, so he did.

As a child, there were two things in my understanding that were permanent. The first was my life. I had no thoughts whatsoever about the possibility of this life coming to an end. The second thing that was permanent was my happiness; I just thought it would be there forever.

But at age three, I was unpleasantly introduced to a much more fickle aspect of my being.

When I touched that hot stove, I came to the quick conclusion that I would do anything in my power to avoid physical pain. Once I came to that conclusion, there was a new addition to the Committee. I felt my Life and Happiness were guaranteed, so all I really had to worry about was avoiding pain. The opposite of pain was pleasure, so Pleasure became my new member. My goal became building up Pleasure.

At that very young point in my life, nothing was more applicable to my everyday activities than Pleasure. Of course, my thinking was very immature, but at the same time practical to every human alive. I wanted to avoid all pain, and the most real pain I could feel was in the physical. So I made my decisions based on which option would create the most pleasure, or the least amount of pain. I didn't touch the stove anymore, because that would create more pain.

At such an early age, I had unknowingly appointed Pleasure to the highest position in my decision-making process. He became the reason I did or did not do things—the chairman of the Committee. "If it feels good, do it," became my motto. Of course, at that age, my parents could still overrule my Committee with the snap of their fingers, and from time to time they even used the power of pain to help with the "overruling process."

Pleasure began ruling the Committee at that early age, and since then, he had only gained power. As I grew older, he became a strong advocate of the party life, because it felt good to get drunk and high. It felt good to be surrounded by friends. It felt good to live immorally. A little partying felt good, and a lot felt better. So motivated by Pleasure, I was partying a lot. It was always a quick-fix to any pain or problem in my life, and there was no one there to deliver spankings anymore.

Pleasure dominated the decision-making, and the other members had little say at all. The meetings were just a formality to doing whatever Pleasure wanted. He didn't like when Conscience ruffled the feathers of his power, but it did nothing he could see to hurt his dictatorship. As the primary director of my existence, Pleasure wanted the meetings to be quick, and everything to stay the same from year to year. As long as he retained his power, everything was great with him. He strongly opposed any suggestion of change.

profile: logic

Logic was an older man of about fifty-five, but his age was deceptive. He was still as fiery and quick-witted as the younger men. His gray hair and beard were medium-length and kept fairly neat, though he occasionally went too long without trimming them. He had small oval glasses, and was concerned only with knowledge—accumulating and processing it. He specialized in making new, useful connections with the facts he had learned. He was renowned within the Committee for his intelligence, and commanded the respect of his peers as a result.

I was introduced to Logic when my parents started to spank me. When I figured out that certain behaviors caused the spankings, I logically stopped those behaviors, and Logic entered the Committee. He had really started to bloom when I was playing with those Legos at around age four. Though other kids had more and better blocks than I did, I made an important realization; I could build anything I wanted with the pieces I had, with the help of Logic. There were so many combinations, and the sky was the limit as far as creativity.

Logic had also been very helpful in introducing the fifth member, Conscience, to the Committee. Once Logic realized that I could avoid the spankings, he also figured out how. All I had to do was pay special attention to what my parents told me, and obey. Conscience developed as I started to listen to their advice and incorporate it into my mentality, if only to avoid the spankings. What else could I do? My parents had complete control of my life. It was going to be a long hard road if I didn't obey.

Since the spankings and the Legos, Logic had built a lot of nice things for me in my life, placing his trust primarily in "the odds." Obeying my parents was logical, because it kept my butt from getting sore. College was a logical choice for me, because it bettered my odds of getting a good job. My professional job was a logical choice, because it set me up to earn money and be successful. I was convinced Logic had an answer for all of life's challenges and decisions.

Logic had input into three different areas in my life. He was first to contribute valuable analytical ability when called upon for the purpose of my job and other complex problems. His second responsibility was decision-making input when multiple factors had to be considered in a life-decision. But his more important role was to make sure I didn't do anything illogical. Logic's natural enemy was ignorance, so any movement based upon ignorance was to be strictly avoided.

Logic was pretty much indifferent to the whole drinking-and-smoking idea. Yeah, it was a little detrimental to my fitness, but I had a good job. I deserved to have a little fun, under his reasoning. He was vigilant for anything too negative, anything overly stupid, but the partying had been "reasonable" to that point. He did notice an ever-so-slight decrease in his quick-wit, and he didn't like the drunk driving but, all things considered, it would be illogical to get worked up about such small issues. He hadn't heard too many complaints, so it was fine by him to continue along this path.

At age four, the Committee rounded out at five members: Life, Happiness, Pleasure, Logic, and Conscience. The simplicity of those early years made them the most joyous of my life. My decisions were easy to make, with the worst possible outcome being a spanking or two. My life would soon get a lot more complicated.

chapter 3: **reality**

By the time I was five years old, I had a decent grasp on walking, talking, and even low levels of analytical thinking. I knew most every nook and cranny of our huge woods house, and also had a good understanding of the parentally-established guidelines that would keep me spanking-free. Operating within these bounds, my three-year-old sister and I either made a selection out of the toy box, or we opted for more physical recreation. Inside the house, we often rode our bikes and other rideable toys through the expansive floor plan. We even had an indoor swing—a dangling rope with a knot and a round board that yielded hours of flying fun. And there were even more options outdoors. We had a pond in which to swim or just play in the mud. We had a huge heap of sand that was to us a glorified sandbox. We had an even bigger swing. We had woods and paths and wildlife to keep us constantly amused. What better play-place could a kid dream about?

As much as I loved to play, I also liked to learn about new ways to play. In observing my two most significant influences at the time, my parents, I noticed that they liked to play too, but their "playing" was different than mine. Along with the construction of the house, my dad had nailed a basketball hoop to a tree in our backyard. For a short time, I quietly watched my parents throw the basketball up into that towering ten-foot hoop, assured that someday I too would be able to do the same. But "someday" seemed so far away, and I wanted to be part of the fun as soon as possible. At age five, I decided to get serious about it.

I interrupted my parents' game, asking them to give me a try—a request they granted. I strained and struggled with all I could to granny-shot that massive ball up at the basket. It was a lot harder than my parents made it look. Over and over, I threw it back into the woods behind the tree. Over and over, they stopped their games to patiently wait for my pathetic shot attempts. It seemed like I would never be able to get the ball into that hoop.

Finally, one day, I did it. When that ball sank through that net for the first time, I felt like I had won the championship of the world. My goal had finally been accomplished, despite all the odds and a 100-percent failure rate prior to that point. After the happiness of that moment died down, I realized I just wanted more. So I kept shooting. Eventually, my aim improved a little, and I moved out further from the basket, and kept at it. Little by little, my basketball ability was increasing.

After a summer of practice, my ability had moved from "none" to "horrible," but I certainly wasn't giving up. The success of making a basket felt so good that it cancelled the failures of the ten or twenty previous misses. But it was time to forget about basketball for a little while and move on to a fresh challenge. It was time for my first day of school.

My parents had signed me up for a small private Baptist school, which was one of my first exposures to the "real world," as sheltered as that exposure was. To that point, I had only known family and my parents' friends, but once I entered school, I had to forge my own relationships. I initially didn't invest much energy into the friendship area; I viewed school as an interruption to my play time. But I did make some interesting discoveries as I examined this new realm of reality. The school building and my new peers didn't use candles for light, and they had a really intriguing device I had seen at my grandma's house called a "TV." I then realized that my parents had played a "cruel trick" on me, and that the house in which we were living didn't have electricity.

The centrally-located stone fireplace kept the "woods house" warm, and candles and kerosene lamps lit our dark halls. Our water source was a hand pump located in the kitchen. To flush the toilet, we just poured a bucket of water into the bowl. Cooking was done on an ancient wood stove, and our perishables were kept in a cooler with ice. As a child, I never really understood why my parents had chosen to go without electricity. It was a unique way to live, but I didn't know any better. It was "normal" to me.

At age five, living without electricity made no difference to me; I got home, and I was back to my playing Legos or action figures or basketball. I didn't need anything more than a stick shaped like a gun, or a ball and a hoop to have fun. So what did I care about electricity? The absence of a television forced me to find other creative ways to occupy my time.

I continued to work on my basketball game each summer growing up. I liked the sport partly because of the fantastic feeling of making a hoop, and partly because my parents liked it so much. It was perfect for family bonding; time after time my mom and dad and I gathered under that backyard hoop. Eventually, by the time I was eight, I decided it was time to step it up a notch. I could shoot, and I could even dribble a little, so it was time for a new challenge. It was time to take on my dad one-on-one. Of course, my dad obviously had to take it easy on me. And though many fathers might contribute a bit of lax defense or a few coaching tips from the sideline, this was not the case with my dad. My only assistance was a few rule modifications. My dad was not allowed to use his arms or hands on defense, and my shots were worth more points than his. Once these rules were in place, the competition began.

Certainly the no-arms rule cut down his blocks-per-game, but it didn't eliminate them. My dad would aggressively defend me, using his face if necessary for blocking my shots. My offensive attacks were not very effective, but my defense was even less. It was quite a challenge for an eight-year-old to guard a full-grown man in the post. I definitely felt discouraged with my inability to compete.

My dad beat me every time we played. But the challenge motivated me. My successes on the court were rare, but they were still there occasionally, in the form of a few points here and there. And "occasionally" was all I needed because the feeling of making a basket was so wonderful.

It was like I had again beaten the odds whenever the ball went through the net. I grew to like that victorious feeling more and more. I started to crave it.

When I turned nine, everything was going peachy in my life. I had established a few friends at school and I was enjoying positive family time at home with my dad, mom, and two sisters. Then one day, the bubble around my little protected life was shattered when a word I had heard before suddenly became much more applicable to my life. Much like "hot," I learned a new and painful definition that made my "reality" even more real. My parents were getting a *divorce*.

My mom took my two sisters and I into a private room of the small Baptist school and broke the news to us. I didn't understand much of what was going on at the time, and I'm sure that my younger sisters understood even less. All I knew was that my heart was breaking. I felt a new pain I had not known much of before—a deep emotional pain. We cried and hugged for a long time, but that pain wouldn't go away.

I was devastated. I just didn't know what to think. I few days earlier, my life was perfect. And now the two people I loved the most didn't love each other anymore. What about all the "God" these two had forced into my life? What about "doing the right thing?" I knew divorce was not the right thing, yet there it was, agonizingly, in front of me. I knew I had to do all I could to stop it. Unfortunately, at age nine, all I could do couldn't stop it. My parents split, and my sisters and I lived with my mom. My dad got visitation on the weekends. I became one of the millions of American children that came from a broken home.

"Broken" was how I felt. A large part of the happiness I knew so well as a child was taken from me during the divorce and its aftermath. But time didn't stop to allow me to gain my bearings; it just kept chugging along. I had to go to school, and I had to go to church, and I had to try to stay happy. Most of my fun activities got put on permanent hold, including basketball. I just didn't feel much like playing anymore.

The divorce left my mom's finances, and indirectly mine and my sisters', in quite a mess. We had to move out of the woods house I loved so much and into a tiny cottage with two small bedrooms—one for me and one for my mom and sisters to share. The water there smelled like rotten eggs and the place was quite rundown. It did have electricity though, which was a whole new world to me and my sisters. Hours spent at play turned to hours spent mesmerized watching our thirteen-inch TV.

As we continued at our small private school, I started to notice that my fellow students had better toys than I did. And that was just the start. They had better houses and yards and bikes than I did too. These things were out of my family's monetary grasp. All of our stuff was hand-me-down, from clothes to furniture to our TV. When other kids were rushing out to get the new Nintendo, my family was extremely thankful to receive someone's old Atari as a gift. And that old Atari certainly got a lot of use. I realized during that time that money had a large part to do with quality of life.

I had a small allowance, and would receive gifts from grandparents for Christmas and my birthday, so I had a little bit of income. I could afford some candy at the corner store, and maybe even an action figure here or there. At first, I spent money when I got it, but later learned the value of saving as I pursued toys bigger than the five-dollar action figures. I first saved up to buy myself a pricey thirty-dollar Lego pirate set. Next on my gratification-delaying list was the amazing feat of saving up for a Gameboy—a ninety-dollar accomplishment. Odd jobs here and there helped me to learn the value of money, and planning around that money.

Eventually, due to finances coupled with our poor living conditions, my family moved from that cottage to a nearby town where my grandparents and great-grandparents lived. At age twelve, this was another devastating twist on my life, as I had established some friendships, including my childhood best friend, at the private school. But I again had no control over this situation, and had to go along with it. My great-grandparents let us move in with them for a while, and my sisters and I began to attend public school when I was in seventh grade.

Public school was a culture-shock for me—yet another blinding dose of reality. I went from a kindergarten-through-twelfth-grade private school of about fifty students to a public school with over four hundred in the seventh grade class alone. When I walked into that school, I was about as uncool as a student could possibly be. Back at the private school, whatever I wore, as long as it was modest, was A-okay. In this public school, I was judged based on clothing, how I talked, and what I was good at. I was completely clueless when it came to popularity, and my ignorance placed me at the very bottom of the "socially-accepted" totem pole. I was one of those kids who would eat my lunch alone at the end of one of the cafeteria tables, hoping no one would give me trouble.

I didn't fit in at all, and I had no idea how to. I was a "nice boy," according to my mother, but that only helped me to get along with teachers. I eventually started to make loose connections with other less-socially-accepted students, but most of the kids never gave me the time of day. I decided I would have to do everything I could to make it into the "cool crowd."

I made some observations, and the first thing I noticed was that the cool kids were swearing. So I integrated swearing into my vocabulary. I noticed that the cool kids wore jeans and T-shirts, so I banned the mom-chosen corduroys and collared shirts from my wardrobe. The cool kids had long, rebellious hair, so I started to grow my hair out. The cool kids listened to loud, often profane, music so I started listening too. The cool kids didn't listen to authority, so I tried that from time to time.

I never achieved coolness in junior high. It was a lot more of a challenge than it seemed. In high school, I rose from the rank of "nobody" to "barely-noticeable nerdy guy." My circle of friends, typically those with comparable low coolness, was growing so I was making progress. But I still struggled to be socially acceptable. I might have been book-smart, but my limited basketball skills and social track record still wouldn't let me fit in.

Late in high school, while pursuing "coolness," I discovered a new aspect of life. I couldn't do much to improve my social status, but I could do something to improve my body. I started to realize the importance of health, and the fact that I had the ability to make my own health better. I began lifting weights a little bit, and as a result, I got stronger and better-defined. I was lifting and playing a lot of basketball, so my muscles and my cardiovascular system were both in good shape. I was strong and could virtually run forever. I graduated high school in excellent shape physically, but still in social disparity. I was undeniably a man, by the official standard. I had gained the judgment, the decision making-process, that I intended to use for the rest of my life, but I still didn't feel complete. I was still searching for something.

I found what I was looking for in college. There I entered a new world where the social slate from my high school days was wiped almost completely clean. I started to meld with a new lifestyle I really hadn't explored much before. I started to get into the party scene. I met my best-friend-and-party-buddy, just as I started to discover what alcohol had for me in life. Shortly after that incorporation, I found pot and its "magical hallucinogenic effects." I thought I was finally in the real world, and I had everything that I ever wanted. I was alive, happy, healthy, cool, and smart. What more could I want?

I studied during the week and binged on the weekends. Then, shifting gears, I started to study during the day and binge during the night. I could always find a group of "friends" that wanted to get drunk or high, and as long as I had some pot or alcohol, my social acceptance continued to rise. Of course, my grades went from impeccable to acceptable, but it didn't matter to me. I was learning the balancing game, holding my partying in one hand and my responsibility in the other. My understanding, based on my limited experience, was that "balance" was the basis of adult life.

My most recent accomplishment had been the return to my hometown after graduating from college. Now I could show that silly little town how cool I had become. And with my new drinking and smoking habits, I was quickly accepted. My professional job further assured others how far I had progressed, and how awesome I felt I was. I believed that I had made the transition to adulthood nearly flawlessly. I continued to juggle the responsible-man image by day and the party-boy by night.

That juggling act took me right up to Christmas, where the responsible side of me had taken over for a little family time. So there I sat, bored at my mom's house, as I collected my gifts and socialized with my family. And there was a lot more family socialization to come throughout that day. *It's going to be hours until I can go back and hang out with my friends,* I thought to myself. It was a simple complaint, but I had to wonder exactly what I meant by the word "friends." I would get drunk or high with anyone. So were my friends the people I hung around, or were my friends the drugs?

profile: competition

Competition was a very interesting character. He was quiet and peaceable most of the time, but he could sure make a scene under the right circumstances. He was about thirty years old, very non-athletic-looking and almost chubby, with brown, curly, unkempt hair and a few days worth of beard. His clothing of choice was old athletic gear, and he favored short jogging shorts and a tight sleeveless tee. Topping off the ensemble was his signature red-white-and-blue headband.

Competition sure wasn't known for his intelligence. But just because he wasn't smart didn't mean he wouldn't surprise you with his ability. To look at him under normal circumstances, or even hear him talk, no one would predict he was of any value to decision-making. But under the right conditions, Competition would take on anybody or anything. Daily living wasn't that challenging, but he lived for those rare moments that it was. Anytime a challenge came along, and he decided to take it, he did everything in his power to accomplish it. He didn't always succeed, but he always gave the coach's cliché "110% effort."

Competition was born as my dad taught me the game of basketball and other games throughout my youth. Success felt great, and winning was the best success around. Nothing was so simple, so cut-and-dried as "I win, you lose." There was no middle-ground. There could be no further dispute over who had played a better game once the final score was in. Competition had developed into a juggernaut in my life, motivating my desire to win at everything from basketball and ping-pong to Monopoly and Euchre.

Competition had a catch-phrase that was a true indicator of his complexity. That phase was "I'm gonna kick your butt," or some "butt-kicking" derivative of it. His services were utilized mainly in playing sports or video-games or cards. Basketball was his hands-down favorite; it was the area in which he truly loved to shine. He felt that after all the failures, and all the practice, he had earned even the limited skills he possessed. And he wanted to show them off. He tried not to be, but he was a little arrogant, proud of his accomplishments on the court. And as long as he was given an allotted time to play basketball, he wasn't going to cause any problems.

Competition wasn't that intelligent, and he wasn't that observant, but he finally began to notice that his basketball time was starting to slip during my partying days. He wasn't really sure why, and he usually listened to the other wiser members, but he was feeling a little frustrated as his time kept getting put on hold. Rarely, he had voiced this frustration, only to be reassured that everything was going well and that he would have more time in the future. He was often given the games that appealed less to him, such as the video or card games, to pacify him. He was usually content with these substitutes, but he was openly convinced to never let anyone take basketball from him.

profile: finance

Finance was the stereotypical businessman. He was a forty-five-year-old man who always wore an expensive black suit, a white shirt, and a bland dark tie. His black hair was slicked back, and showed signs of graying on the sides. He wore thick plastic-rimmed glasses that were always sliding down his nose. He normally carried a nice leather briefcase in one hand, and some sort of financial newspaper in the other. There wasn't one moment of the day that he didn't look busy.

Finance became a part of my life when I discovered the value of money, and how it could be used to improve the quality of my life. Things I wanted, or thought I wanted, fell into place when proper spending was applied. I could own anything if I applied Finance's principles. And what I had initially wanted was my independence, so Finance helped me to achieve it.

Finance's goal was to make sound decisions regarding income and employment. He was quite pleased with the professionalism and paycheck of my job, though the spending patterns and my shoddy work attendance concerned him a little. Still, he was satisfied to stay out of the conflicts as long as money was coming in and properly allocated to expenses first. Saving would be great, but he was a great believer in "chance." And chances were that if he raised a stink about savings, some other financial area would struggle. So he decided to keep the status quo going for as long as possible. He knew my party budget was excessive, but he wasn't going to cause problems unless he noticed a serious turn for the worst.

Society was "Mr. Cool." He always wore a different outfit, usually a socially-safe button-down shirt or a sweater, and baggy jeans or khakis. He was young, around twenty, and his hair was gelled with the bed-head look, and sometimes a baseball cap. He was clean-shaven and very stylish. He spoke well, and he was witty and intelligent, though he was also a little stuck-up and shallow. He was very good friends with the chairman, Pleasure.

I was introduced to Society in junior high. He was at first very cruel to me, but there was something about social acceptance that he made me want. I wanted to be the one deciding what was cool, not just following the crowd. But Society was convinced that the key to being accepted was to mimic those who had acceptance. My popularity-achieving charade began then, and it continued throughout high school and college. Society was the voice of everyone around me, including those who didn't necessarily have any connection to me. In fact, Society got most of his input from people who didn't care about me at all.

Society was in charge of my social image. He let me know what was cool to wear, to drink, and to do. He let me know which girls I should hit on, and which I should avoid, simply by applying social standards. Though he specialized in the party end of my activities, he was also useful in the professional sector. There, again, the mimicry achieved a level of notoriety for me, although spill-over from the partying often threatened my professional image. But for the most part, I knew what to do just by following the example of my coworkers.

Society loved the party scene. Within a drunken haze, the constraints of the social atmosphere felt less binding. Anything was cool, socially okay, if I was drunk enough. Society said it was okay to be a fool then, and to make silly choices. My drunken party buddies and I could let down our social guards and feel freedom in the knowledge that most anything we did was socially acceptable. As far as Society could tell, my life was going masterfully, according to his social plan. I was just the person Society wanted me to be.

profile: health

Health was a fitness nut. He was about twenty-five and had a homely face with an oblong head, shaved completely bald. He typically wore wind-pants and a tank-top that showed off his fine physique. He was lean and muscular, and was regarded as kind of a meat-head, for all "practical purposes." But he knew his stuff when it came to the gym, and he was also well-versed in dietary trivia. He was a nice guy, a little high-strung, but personable. Get him talking about fitness, and he'd never shut up.

Health became a small part of my life when I began to see the connections between working out and good health, back in high school. It wasn't until later, as the partying took over in college, that I actually noticed some of the negative effects of poor health decisions. At that point, I began to pay a little more attention to Health. As my physical condition began to deteriorate, mostly due to smoking and drinking, I was forced to listen to his hints for healthy living.

Health's number-one goal was to keep me from becoming lethargic and inactive. This seemed simple enough, but he was beginning to lose the battle against the unhealthy lifestyle of drinking and smoking. He conceded that a beer a day was said to be good for the body, but not twelve or eighteen. And the smoking—both pot and cigarettes—was downright hypocrisy to healthy living. He had been satisfied to keep his mouth shut as long as time was given to working out, but he was losing ground there too. He was growing tired of his diminishing influence, and he had previously voiced his concern that some sort of change had to take place. He didn't get to speak out at the meetings too often, on account of his "muscle-head" reputation, but he was looking for a chance to emphasize his message.

At age twenty-two, my Committee was complete, as far as I was concerned. I had nine influences that directed my path: Life, Happiness, Pleasure, Logic, Conscience, Competition, Finance, Society, and Health. Chairman Pleasure led the way, strongly supported by Society and Logic. The other members tried to hold on to their feeble positions, most of them intimidated by the dictatorship of Pleasure.

Pleasure didn't like the bureaucracy of the Committee, mainly because it cramped his fun. He contended that most decisions in the course of living were simple enough to be determined out-of-committee. In other words, Finance made financial decisions, Health made fitness decisions, and so on, and meetings were often not necessary. But at the request of the rest of the Committee,

Pleasure had agreed to periodic meetings, usually every six months, to discuss the status of the members and any needed changes. Beyond that, Pleasure wanted the meetings to be as infrequent as possible, and he got his way due to his strong influence.

Between the scheduled status meetings, the members continued to regulate their particular areas, remaining vigilant for arising problems or issues that may require discussion at the next meeting. If a member noticed a problem, the first step was to notify the Committee. The second step was to gather evidence to verify that the problem existed. The third step was to come up with possible solutions, and gather information on those solutions. The final step was to implement the proper solution and eliminate the problem. Conscience was at step one with his Christmas complaint.

chapter 4: **decline**

'd like to say that my Christmas-time concern made me stop dead in my tracks and change my ways, never to smoke or drink again. But the fact of the matter was that I didn't like that little voice telling me I was wrong. Who wants a party-pooper like that riding their back? My first instinct was to fight back against this new intruder to my fun and independence, and my weapons of choice were pot and alcohol. Suppressing my conscience seemed to work for a little while. Initially, I wouldn't even admit that there was a problem—"classic denial." I did make the compromise that I would keep my eyes and ears alert in case I discovered one. I decided to become conscious of what my partying was doing for me, both positively and negatively. I was confident that the positive would easily outweigh the negative.

I tried to be impartial, but at first there didn't seem to be any negatives. I had been partying in conjunction with "the responsible life" for quite a while. I could still work, go to the gym, and fulfill family obligations, on top of my "letting loose" in the evenings. Anything negative, I originally concluded, was so insignificant that it didn't even matter. I didn't realize that the subtlety of the negative was exactly what made drinking and drugging so dangerous.

As a child, I had decided that I never wanted to drink in my life. I had apparently paid real good attention to some sermon on "the evilness of drunkards," and determined that drinking wasn't for me. I also remember a time in my life that I thought people who smoked pot were the scum of society—useless and hopeless. I'm sure my parents and the anti-drug campaign commercials both contributed to these incorrect stereotypes. I had thought that if I drank or smoked pot, I would be instantly addicted and my life would fall apart in a matter of hours. But one night later in life, as peer pressure coupled with my desire to be independent, I went to a party and did a little drinking. The next morning, I recounted the events of the previous evening, and concluded that I had fun. I also noticed my life was fully intact, contrary to my preconception. If my parents were wrong about this, what else were they wrong about? So a little while later, while drunk, I tried a little pot, and again found no apparent negatives. Both drugs gave me a new feeling that standard life didn't seem to provide, with minimal consequence. The stresses of everyday life seemed to disappear when I was under the influence.

But the consequences of drinking and pot-smoking were definitely there, hiding beneath the positives, and after the Christmas of 2001, I finally began to see them. I was spending a lot of money and a lot of time supporting my partying. This left me with less money for necessities, and less time for exercise and basketball. My job attendance and work quality were slipping. I was becoming unhealthy, and my dependence on the drugs was increasing. I woke up nearly every morning feeling weak and ill, hung over from the night before. Mentally, I was also in a state of decline. I was not as quick-witted as before. If I encountered a problem that required some strategizing, I would usually give up or use trial-and-error before I would try to think it out. My memory started to diminish, and from time to time I wouldn't even be able to remember certain pieces of the previous night. I lost much of my confidence when dealing with the professional coworkers and clients at my job, afraid my brain was just going to "lock-up" on me. Basically, I was getting dumber.

I was sure that all of these physical and mental symptoms could be found in an anti-drug brochure somewhere, but they became a little more real when I actually began to experience them. I wasn't just a social drinker anymore, I concluded as I sat alone in my apartment getting drunk and high. Left with my thoughts and my intoxication, I started to realize what my friends had distracted me from. I really didn't like these drugs anymore. Sure, I enjoyed the buzz, but I didn't like what they were taking away from me. Something was wrong, and I couldn't deny it. Pieces of my life that were really important to me were beginning to slowly disintegrate. When I finally weighed out the positives and negatives, I began to get a clearer understanding of what I had to do. When something was wrong, it had to be corrected. I had to eliminate the cause of the problem. I had to stop the partying.

I had previously admitted to myself and my friends that I would probably be drinking and smoking dope all my life. But I began to understand that the quality of my life would continue to diminish if I kept on that track. So I made a passive decision to quit. Someday. Having made that decision, I could justify some more partying, since "it would all be coming to a close soon." But quitting, and even cutting back, proved to be a little harder than just making the decision. I decided to quit, then I got tanked for two weeks straight. *Hmmm... that didn't work,* I told myself. *I'd better try harder.* So I quit again. And then I started again. One day I quit for good. The next day, I started again. I quit then restarted, quit then restarted, often with just hours between my decision and failure. Repetitious failures left me daunted, and I considered the possibility that quitting was not an option. So I returned to my vices, allowing them to squeeze more and more life from me.

During the spring of 2002, I kept gearing up, trying to really motivate myself to stop, only to fail again. I decided to incorporate a new approach; I would quit one, then the other. That way, I could at least eliminate the illegal one, weed, and then proceed to work on the more socially-acceptable problem of drinking. This strategy also met monumental failure, and I realized that alcohol and weed were working hand-in-hand with each other in not allowing me to quit. If I could barely resist smoking pot when I was sober, how was I going to resist when I was drunk? I couldn't, and I realized that I would have to quit both simultaneously in order to have a chance.

I continued to focus some of my energy on cutting back as the summer approached. I really made an honest effort, but fouled it up nearly daily. I made legitimate attempts to put a little distance between myself and the friends who so easily distracted me, again having minimal success. Though I still hung around my best-friend-and-drinking-buddy almost every day, I forced myself to head home at more decent hours of the night, trying to trump up some discipline. In his late-night travels without me, he came across a new group of friends.

He was spending a lot of his time with a group of girls, who were a lot less into the party crowd than we were, but still liked to get high or drink a little from time to time. Up until that point, most of our cronies had been guys who liked to get all drunk and act like morons. But girls changed everything. I was trying to be responsible with my life and drinking, but one of the girls in this group caught my eye. In high school, we had worked together at McDonald's, and had become good friends. I had always had a little crush on her, but had found pursuing it a near impossibility with her boyfriend in the scene. So we had flirted and had fun together, with nothing ever becoming of it. Now, years later, she had returned home from college for the summer, and we were both single. So we again began to have fun together. We both enjoyed each other's company, and we both enjoyed smoking pot.

One night, at her friend's house, circumstances worked out just right. Her friend left and wasn't going to be home until the next morning. So we smoked a little pot together, and then we both "got tired." One of us made the bold suggestion that we go to bed in the guest room. That night, we became more than good friends.

The next morning, someone was banging on the door, so I got up and answered it. That's how I officially met her mom—caught red-handed. My "new girlfriend" came out of the bedroom, and we all had a lovely chat. I was just sitting there thinking... *Where is this going?* The physical aspects seemed great, but I had no idea where it left "us." Later, after her mom left, I talked with this girl, and we decided to just "play it by ear"—essentially to continue the intimacy with no real commitment. And so we did; some nights I was with her, some nights I was with someone else. Most nights, I was alone.

The casualty of my new female focus was my drug-quitting attempts; I completely forgot about them. Instead, I did what I wanted, and whatever pleased me most. The negative consequences continued to mount, but sex completely distracted me from them. It was like something knew I was on the right track, and threw me an additional bonus to keep me content with the party life. And it worked, but there was still something out-of-whack with my happiness.

date: june 2, 2002
purpose: six-month review
agenda: status reports, happiness slump

The members of the Committee sat around the table in the boardroom for the six-month review, to deliberate on my condition and formulate a new way to revitalize Happiness. Conscience's "outburst" at the last meeting had created a little controversy, but things had calmed down since then. Many of the members, like Finance, Competition, and Logic, reported that things were "adequate," and nothing better. Pleasure, however, was at an all-time high. For the first time in a long time, Happiness piped up from his seat on the Committee, before the chairman could even call the meeting to order. The board members looked toward the boy, surprised to hear from a voice they barely recognized anymore.

"You guys are always talking about business, but I wanna do somethin' fun," he boldly stated. "I'm sick of these stupid meetings, and I don't wanna come anymore."

"Well, I guess nobody's twisting your arm, little guy," replied Chairman Pleasure, slightly annoyed. "I'd like to call this meeting to order..."

"Don't listen to him, Happiness," said Life. "We love having you around. What can we do to make things better?"

"I dunno," said Happiness indecisively. "Somethin'."

"Great," said Pleasure disgusted, "you and Conscience both, making waves, trying to change 'somethin'.' We need a proposition for change, not just some obscure observation. I think these meetings are as dull as you do, Happiness, but your complaining just makes them longer."

"Go easy on him," said Life defensively. "He's just as entitled to speak as anyone. And I think he's right; I propose that we reduce the time wasted partying."

"We gotta do something different!" exclaimed Happiness, near tears. To the surprise of Pleasure, some of the other members nodded in either agreement or sympathy.

"Okay, okay, guys," said Pleasure. "You want a change? You want to please the little guy here? I have the perfect solution. We'll get you a little playmate. A little girlfriend. We can get that cute little female, you know the one, who you can frolic around with, and maybe it will help you to feel better if we secure a relationship with her. How does that sound?"

"Well, I guess it might help to have someone around," said Happiness timidly.

"Okay, so that will be the first of our objectives for the second half of the year," said Pleasure. "Heck, she might be good for a few things beyond that, who knows?" he said, winking at Society before moving on. "The next order of business is a change *I* would like to institute. Now I have been sensing a little unrest among the members, so I have devised a new plan that will alleviate some of that. My plan is regarding our current method of transportation. I think we all agree that the Colt Vista is an eyesore. So my plan is to ditch that thing and get something sweet, something we can really enjoy. After all, we deserve it."

"What exactly do we deserve?" asked Life analytically.

"We deserve the best we can afford," said Pleasure, growing excited with the idea. "Let's throw a little monetary clout around, get something really nice, like a big sport utility vehicle."

"Sounds great to me, man," responded Society.

"I don't think it's such a great idea to be spread so thin financially," said Finance doubtfully.

"I don't think you understand what kind of change we need, Mr. Chairman," added Life.

"Well, then why don't you tell me, wise Life," said Pleasure condescendingly. "What change do we need?"

"The problem is the partying," replied Life. "It's eating up too much time, money, and health. We have to get rid of it."

"Oh, now you're just being silly," said Pleasure. "Drinking is what adults do. You want to take that away from us, revert to a time of straight-laced discipline without any fun or friends? And pot, well, that's a nice little rebellious twist in the party scene, and has also brought its share of new friends into our circle. And you want to ditch them? You'll never get my approval on that. In other words, it's not going to happen."

"The rest of you know what I mean, don't you?" asked Life, looking around the table. The other members looked around awkwardly trying to ignore him, intimidated by Pleasure.

"I know what you mean," said Conscience meekly.

"Me too," said Happiness.

"You shut up, Happiness," commanded Pleasure. "I'm getting you a playmate, the least you could do is show me some respect. And Conscience, I expect some rocking-the-boat out of you, as a useless old fuddy-dudd. But Life, we've always been on good terms. Why this uproar now?"

"We have to do what's best for the Committee as a whole, not just you," replied Life.

"Why don't you trust my leadership?" asked Pleasure. "I've brought us this far."

"*We've* brought us this far, it wasn't all you," answered Life. "And *we* need to quit with the drinking and pot and cigarettes."

"Okay, if you're going to stir up problems, I'll make you a deal," said Pleasure. "You and the 'moron squad'," he gestured toward Happiness and Conscience, "can try to come up with a plan for quitting, and present it at our next meeting. And I get to go buy the vehicle of my dreams."

"Um..." began Finance.

"Shut up!" said Pleasure quickly, glaring at him. "Just shut up." Pleasure turned his attention back to Life. "I know you've been thinking about it, Life. I even know you've tried to stop the partying against my will in the past. But I'm not going to get mad. Heck, if you agree to that new car, you can continue to try to institute your quitting programs before the next meeting. I don't even care."

Life pondered the decision for a moment. He looked around the table, thought for another second or two, and said "Deal."

"Alright then!" exclaimed Pleasure excitedly. "Meeting adjourned. Good luck with the quitting, chump," he said to Life arrogantly as he walked out of the boardroom. "Just remember, you can quit anytime you want..." Pleasure mocked.

The other members sat around the table with a quiet awkwardness, watching Life curiously. He stood up with a smile of contentment on his face, acknowledged the members with a grin and a nod, and walked out the door. The other members dispersed in quiet wonderment, confused by Pleasure's willingness to negotiate.

chapter 5: **the fantastic expedition**

Early in the summer of 2002, my casual partner and I became "exclusive," building our relationship with more time, physicality, and weed. She was a joyous girl, and had a child-like happiness about her. She brought me companionship and physical satisfaction, and went part of the way to filling the void in my happiness. She could get lost in nature, or music, or art, mesmerized and focused much like I remember being when I played with my blocks as a child. I often wrote it off as immaturity, as she seemed oblivious to the "real world" and what I thought was important in life. Realistically, we both had a lot of growing up to do, but regardless, her child-like mentality had a way of calming me and making me happy, or at least helping me to remember what happiness was like.

I decided that my Colt Vista van-car was not projecting the social image I was looking for in a vehicle, so I went down to the local dealership to see what kind of options I had. I wanted something that said "I am awesome" to everyone who saw it. A beautiful dark-blue SUV caught my attention.

The truck was a Ford Expedition, a large vehicle that had "prestige" written all over it. I saw it, and my mind was instantly made. I took it on a test drive over to some friends' house, and their reaction confirmed my decision. All I had to do was hack through the financial red tape, and that baby was mine. I got the biggest loan my bank would give me, with lofty monthly payments, and traded in my grandma's old car. Suddenly, I was cruising the streets of Alpena with new pride.

I had my new girl, and I had my new ride, and things were looking up. And with things looking up, the idea of quitting my partying ways was distant. I continued my drinking and smoking throughout the summer of 2002 and into the fall. But my life still didn't feel complete. My conscience was still bugging me. Eventually, I was more and more aware that my happiness may have been temporarily pacified with these new acquisitions, but it was not growing at all. In fact, it was once again on the decline.

Happiness dissipating, and my drinking and smoking at full-power, I once again concluded that a change had to be made. This time, as I weighed my options for eliminating my habits, I considered a support group, like Alcoholics Anonymous. *Maybe something like that would help,* I thought, but my pride held me back. I just wanted to keep my continuing problem a secret from the world. I didn't want to show any weakness or vulnerability by turning anywhere for help. So a new possible help-source came to mind.

Maybe "God" could help me out. The only problem was that I didn't know if he even existed. God's existence had always been a popular topic of debate in my circle of friends. We would get high and dive into philosophy, debating human origins or a supreme being or supernatural powers. My best friend and I went back and forth on God's existence often. My position was always that he did exist, whereas my friend was an atheist. We had some interesting conversations, and really felt like we were making mind-blowing revelations. We never reached any agreeable conclusion on the matter, but we didn't care. After all, we were just debating for fun.

I chose the "God exists" side of the argument because I knew a lot of God trivia. My parent's church and the private Baptist school of my elementary years gave me a plethora of memorized facts. After my parents' divorce, my mom had started to re-attend my grandparent's Lutheran church—the same one I had "enjoyed" so much the past Christmas Eve. My dad had returned to his Pentecostal church—the denomination that has a reputation for clapping and dancing and speaking in tongues. It had been an interesting mix for me as a teenager; one Sunday in deathly-quiet church, and the next in lunatic church. So over the years, I had seen a lot of "God variety." I knew all about the Bible stories like David and Goliath or Moses and the Red Sea. I even knew some Bible verses I had been forced to learn as a child. I knew about God, but I certainly didn't choose to live how the Bible told me to, or the ways my parents' churches had prescribed. With the independence of my college years, I had dropped completely out of church attendance, and off God's radar, as far as I was concerned.

But as I was considering my party-induced dilemma, I remembered how my parents had described God as a source of help in time of trouble. They really bought into the whole church thing, as indicated by their continued regular attendance. They gave their time, and even money, to the church and its functions, which seemed ludicrous to me. But I was definitely having trouble with my quitting, and so I decided to give God a shot. Nothing serious, I just started to pray from time to time. Maybe he could help me out.

My prayers usually started something like this: "If you exist, God, show me..." or "You mind helping me out a little here... ?" I didn't use all the "thee's" and "thou's" I heard in church, I just made a few simple plain-English requests. I had nothing to lose but the fifteen seconds it took to pray.

In the midst of my new "does-God-exist program," I was also facing some housing issues. Two main factors convinced me that I should move out of my apartment. First, I was in a financial hole because of the Expedition, and needed to find a way to cut costs of living. Second, my apartment was kind of a party hot-spot; people were constantly stopping by looking to party or buy drugs. I knew this was not a good influence on my ability to quit. So I considered my options.

A close friend of mine, and party buddy, was looking for a roommate. The price was right, so I moved in with him for a brief period before I realized responsible living was not going to commence in a house that partied to all hours of the night. Living there did help to defray some of the cost of small claims court, which is where my previous landlord promptly took me when he discovered the condition in which I had left his apartment. But overall, the bad influence of the new party house was not worth the savings, and I was considering other options within a week of moving in.

My dad presented me with a decent proposal. My grandma had recently moved to a care home, and her house was sitting vacant out in the country about a half hour from town. My dad offered to let me stay there, and all I would have to pay was bills—no rent. The drive was a little unappealing, especially with my gas-guzzling Expedition, but all things considered I took the offer. I began to live at my grandma's house early in the fall of 2002.

I was doing a lot of driving at that point in my life. I had a half-hour commute one-way for work each day, and most weekends I was driving down to see my girlfriend, who had returned to her college four hours away. But I didn't mind, with such a sweet ride. I loved to show my truck off around town and downstate with my girlfriend where my partying raged. She expressed some objection to my getting hammered so much, so I tried to tone it down a little for her, but the problem still loomed in my life.

One Friday morning in October of 2002, I was driving my Expedition into town for work, daydreaming about how I was going to go downstate after work for some pleasure and partying. I made sure I had enough pot left in my bag so we could have a great time. I was jammin' out to some blaring "gangsta rap," when suddenly there was a deer in the road, threatening to mess up the grill of my beautiful SUV. I swerved to miss the deer, only to find myself flying through the ditch at about 65 mph, cruise control still on, and absolutely no control of the vehicle. I could see a telephone pole approaching fast, so I cut the wheel hard to miss it. This evasive maneuver caused my truck to turn sideways and begin to roll. It seemed to happen in slow motion. I felt the truck starting to turn over for the first time, and I held the steering wheel tightly with both hands, pressing myself back into the seat so I wouldn't get jerked around or thrown from the vehicle. The windows all blew out on the first roll, showering me with glass. I was just hoping I wasn't going to roll over something, a tree or a branch, that could come through a window and impale me. The second roll threw the contents my Expedition out of the windows into the ditch—my CDs, sports gear, everything. Everything but me. The truck came to a halt right-side-up, and after a few seconds, my CD player came back on, blaring the profane lyrics of my music. I sat there stunned.

The first thing my mind did was go through an inventory checklist. One, am I alive? Yep. Two, is there anything physically wrong with me? I noticed a little blood on my forehead, but nothing major as far as I could tell. And then my mind moved on to damage control. I looked back to see all my stuff, most of it destroyed by the accident. I went to get out, assessing the vehicle, but my door wouldn't open; it had been sealed shut by the rolling. I climbed out the window, and my suspicions were confirmed that the truck was in pretty rough shape. The only thing that wasn't damaged was the front grill that I had swerved so furiously to protect. "Great, now how am I going to go downstate this weekend?" I asked myself.

My Expedition had landed right-side-up in the driveway of a farmhouse, directly in front of the garage. Across the street, I saw a woman looking out her front door, so I headed over to ask if I could use her phone. From there, I called the police, and let my boss know I probably wasn't going to make it in that day. Then I called my dad to come pick me up. Eventually, I remembered that my pot was still in the truck, so I headed back across the street and climbed back in to get my bag out of my center console. I hid it in my shoe and prepared for the arrival of the police.

The accident didn't start to sink in until I was sitting there waiting for the cops and my dad. This was one of those near-death experiences that made a person consider the value of life. I began to wonder about the accident. I had been asking God to show that he existed; was this his way of trying to get through to me? No, I decided, why would he use calamity? But then I started to consider the fact that I might not listen to anything else. If my life was going marvelously, I probably never would have asked God to show up in the first place. If he had been showing me he existed by showering me with happiness even when I was doing the wrong things, would I ever attempt to improve? Or recognize his handiwork? No, if God was going to get my attention or make me think, it would have to be through tragedy. So maybe it was God.

Eventually, a policeman arrived and took the report, and my dad showed up on the scene. He took one look at my demolished truck and gave me a huge hug and began crying, saying how happy he was that I was okay. I supposed my life was worth something to him as well as to me. I decided that I would have to do a lot more thinking about God before I would reach any conclusion. I also decided that I would have to find a new way to visit my girlfriend and my addictions downstate, now that my primary transportation was trashed.

date: october 4, 2002
purpose: emergency meeting
agenda: the roll-over accident

Pleasure had masterminded the girlfriend idea, because he was well aware of the physical pleasure she would bring. He was also aware of the growing unrest within the Committee, and typically tried to put off worrying about it by throwing new factors into the mix, such as the girlfriend or the Expedition. And often, the other members left him alone if he tossed them pacifiers, mainly because of his powerful position as chairman. Who could stand up against over seventeen years of leadership?

With my truck sitting totaled at the conclusion of that wild ride through the ditch, I called an emergency meeting. The Committee came together to discuss the ongoing question, "What are we going to do?" A death-tempting roll-over accident really had the ability to get me thinking. My first thought was that I could have died. And when I thought of death, I thought of Life.

"Well," began Life, "what did you all think of that?"

The members murmured amongst themselves, but Pleasure spoke up quickly. "I thought that was a crazy ride! Holy crap, man, we were flyin' through that ditch! I was getting a little nervous there. No big deal, everything worked out okay. Now we've got to figure out how we're going to get downstate to visit the girlfriend."

"Whoa, whoa, hold up there," interrupted Life. "We're not going to just skim over this like nothing happened. We almost lost everything today. Our entire existence was almost wiped off the planet."

"Almost," agreed Pleasure, playing it off, "but I'd just kinda like to forget about it."

"We can't just forget everything unpleasant that happens," objected Life. "Otherwise, we'd still be touching hot stoves. We need to learn from this experience. You all know that I've been doing a little looking into this 'God' that Mom and Dad couldn't stop talking about. Maybe he's trying to let us know he's out there."

"Are you kidding me?" asked Pleasure cynically. "A little shake-up and you're ready to turn tail and start believing in magic? I've always led this group well, and I assure you that we're okay. Besides, what made you get so bold all of a sudden, Life? I run the show here, in case you forgot. Now let's focus our ability on the real issue, and try to find a way downstate."

"The 'real issue' is going downstate?" asked Life surprised. "How can you even think about that? I think our continued well-being is more critical than temporary fun."

"Maybe Life is right," chimed in Finance. "It was definitely unacceptable to spread finances so thin, and maybe this is an indication of that foolishness. It could be divine, who knows?"

"Accidents happen every day across the globe," said Pleasure. "And this one means something special? I don't think so. Now I won't ask again, let's focus here."

"Maybe we needed 'a spanking'," said Life, "from a higher source..."

"What do you want from me, Life?" asked Pleasure impatiently. "What do you want me to tell you?"

"Well," began Life, "you know that Conscience and Happiness and I have been looking into quitting this party lifestyle, and have even tried to implement a few programs, which have failed miserably mainly due to your resistance."

"Yes, and I intend to continue that resistance if you keep trying to take away my fun," answered Pleasure. "You can't win this one, but go ahead and try if you must. You're wasting your energy though."

"Well, I have another proposal for you," said Life. "And it may be mutually beneficial."

"Okay, I'm listening," said Pleasure. "Spit it out."

"I propose that we move away from Alpena, our hometown," said Life.

"You must be crazy," said Society disgusted. "Tell him he's crazy, Mr. Chairman! We just got back a little over a year ago!" Many of the members stood up, also voicing strong disagreement to such an idea, but Pleasure quickly quieted them.

"That's quite an idea, Life," said Pleasure, stroking his chin. "I don't think the Committee likes it, and I don't either. But what are you offering? What do I get out of the deal if I agree? It better be good."

Life paused for a moment, contemplating before he spoke. "Name it," he finally said hesitantly.

"Are you serious?" asked Pleasure, surprised.

"You can think about it until the year-end meeting," answered Life, "and present your demands then. We will continue as-is until that time, at which point we will determine if a move can be compromised, and discuss my findings on God."

"Fair enough," said Pleasure, imagining the possibilities. "And now we can focus on more pressing matters?"

"Yes," sighed Life.

"The first matter of business is getting downstate," started Pleasure. "I'm sure someone will loan us a car for the weekend, so let's start to look for someone willing."

Pleasure got no resistance for that idea, though many of the members still questioned his priorities.

"The second order of business is that we must soon buy a new vehicle to replace the loss," said Pleasure. "I propose another SUV, something big and nice, like the Expedition. I really liked that ride." The members again kept quiet.

"I don't think that's such a great idea," said Life, speaking for some of the intimidated members. "We need to be a little more intelligent with our purchases. That truck nearly broke the bank for us, and you want to do it again?" Life received many subtle nods.

"Dang," said Pleasure irritated. "You are just raining all over my parade, aren't you? I'm getting a little tired of it. So what do you fun-stoppers want? A Geo?"

"This Committee is assembled for the sake of compromise," said Life. "We just need to find something that's middle-quality and decently priced, that's all." Again, many members, too scared to speak up, nodded agreement.

"Fine," said Pleasure angrily. "We'll find a 'decently-priced' car that makes us feel like paupers. Now can we get out of here and get working on going downstate for the weekend?"

No one put up a fuss, and the meeting was adjourned, with the next scheduled meeting for the year-end.

chapter 6: **monotony**

The Friday of my roll-over accident, I made it an immediate priority to find a way downstate to see my girlfriend. Playing the sympathy card repetitively was finally successful when I explained the accident to my girlfriend's parents. After a little smooth-talking, exaggerating my "great desire to see their wonderful daughter," they let me take their Dodge Neon for the weekend. I promptly headed out of town for a couple nights of partying. Such a "traumatic accident" was a great excuse to get wasted for two days straight. Sunday night, I returned home, and prepped for another monotonous work-week.

Wrecking my Expedition really left me thinking. Maybe I needed a different kind of change in my life. The new truck, which I had driven for only three months, had been an addition, but maybe I needed a subtraction. I was having a pretty tough time subtracting alcohol and weed, so I considered subtracting some of my other negative influences; specifically, the hometown crowd that supported my partying lifestyle.

My accident not only opened new avenues of thinking, but it also created a lot of paperwork. The first thing I had to deal with was the body shop, which quickly confirmed that I had totaled the vehicle, never to be driven again. I then had to deal with my insurance company, which provided me with a pleasant surprise. They had calculated the value of my vehicle to be much greater than I had paid for it three months earlier. I made arrangements with the bank, paying off the Expedition and setting up another loan for my replacement-vehicle purchase. When all the insurance and bank transactions were completed, I essentially walked away from the crash with $4,500 extra cash.

I knew I had to find a lot more responsible use for my money than the purchase of my extravagant truck. And I still couldn't help wondering if God had anything to do with the accident. So I decided to make a political move, "play the odds," and attempt to appease this God if he existed by showing support for my local church. I didn't set foot in the building, but I sent my dad a check for a little of the money I had made on the insurance deal, requesting that he give it to the church. After all, I could afford it, and maybe if God was trying to bug me, I could buy him off.

I also selected my replacement car; this time it was a much more economically-chosen used Grand Am, at less than half the price of the Expedition. I could afford this fairly easily with the retention of my professional job. I tried again to cut back on the party life, sometimes successfully, sometimes not. But I still couldn't shake the thought that further change was in order. I continued to think on it during the fall of 2002, even opening the

Bible from time to time, looking for some insight. The book seemed a lot more complicated and daunting than the stories I remembered from my childhood, and I didn't really get much from it.

I thought back to those "God debates" that my best friend and I had together. He had recently moved downstate, closer to his girlfriend's college, so I didn't talk to him as much anymore. Though neither of us ever "won" our debates, I respected his intelligence, and he respected mine. In fact, he respected my opinion more than most professing "God-supporters," for one reason: I was admittedly headed to hell. Most of our friends did whatever they wanted, immoral or not, and still said, "Sure, I'm going to heaven." But I argued for morals that I did not live by, for principles that were above my own. I argued that God existed, but I certainly wasn't living my life for his program, and the biblical result would be hell. It was a dangerous admission, if God existed, but I didn't really know what I believed at the time of the debates. And I still didn't know what I believed after the roll-over. I was keeping the debate alive internally as I continued to wonder about God.

With my Grand Am, car payments and gas mileage were very affordable, so I had no reason to worry about money. I continued to make the trip downstate to see my girlfriend nearly every weekend, occasionally visiting my best friend too. He only lived about an hour away from her. Every time I went downstate, I had a nice bundle of cash with me, for alcohol, and a nice bundle of weed with me as well. I stayed semi-responsible during the week, sometimes going a few days without drinking, but I got trashed every weekend.

On one of my trips to see my girlfriend, I got pulled over for speeding. I had received speeding tickets before, but that day I happened to have several bags of pot in my center console. Multiple bags constituted drug-dealing charges, if caught, but I just didn't want to mix my high-grade pot and the mids together. All I had to do was stay cool, which I did, accepting the ticket with a nervous smile. But as I pulled away, the thought crossed my mind, *What if I got caught?* Once I reached my destination, I quickly erased that concern with a joint from the high-grade bag.

My life was feeling more and more incomplete as the holiday season was again approaching. Though I was making changes, nothing was changing. I couldn't find happiness in my friends or my girlfriend or my drugs. I really didn't know where else to look. My friends and girlfriend had brought me distraction, at best. My addictions were slowly bringing me down—insurmountable foes. My quitting attempts had brought me failure. I had to change something.

date: december 1, 2002
purpose: twelve-month review
agenda: status reports, upcoming year change
and planning

Pleasure had established his dominance on the Committee, and the previously silent observers, Life and Happiness, had been speaking up after years of dormancy. The recent addiction-related trials I had been experiencing and succumbing to had most of the members up in arms and ready for change. The year-end meeting came together a little early that year, regarding more change and what form it would take, especially as it related to the "moving proposal."

No member wanted to be left out of this meeting, as the impact of recent events had in some way affected everyone. Each member seemed anxious to voice his opinion in light of the accident and the insurance money, and possibilities for change. Life had suggested that each member be given the floor for a few minutes to express themselves. Pleasure didn't like the idea, but the influence of the other members was growing, so he consented.

"I call this meeting to order," announced Chairman Pleasure. "Now let's talk about that move! I've come up with some great ideas..."

"Hold on," said Life boldly. "Let's begin with the status reports, as is protocol."

"How much more of this disrespect do you think I'm going to tolerate, Life?" asked Pleasure threateningly. "Fine, Life, go right ahead..."

Life began. "As most of you know, I have been looking into some new options for change, the first being this resource introduced by Mom and Dad, the entity known as 'God.' I am currently piecing together what we learned during childhood and what we know now to try to determine if he exists as a viable option. I am also doing research into how choosing his ways would affect us, and what we would have to do, as specified in the Bible. I know a lot of people have said a lot of things about his way, and made a lot of promises that don't even seem possible. But at this point, debating Creation or where we go after death is of little value to helping us out of our current situation. Don't let anyone fool you, the matter of the drugs and alcohol is urgent, and a decision is required soon. Most of the information I have collected presents God as a great source of help in time of trouble, but again, we have to determine if he exists. I believe that he does."

"Oh, please..." started Pleasure, irritated. "Urgent?"

"They have a right to hear it, and decide," returned Life. "I want to hear each of your input on the matter. Let's start with Finance."

Invigorated by Life's recent defiance, Finance began. "You all know money has been dwindling, in my belief due to poor spending habits," he said, glancing at Pleasure, then looking down. "I tried to warn you all about the Expedition, and that we couldn't afford it, and hopefully we learned a thing or two when our finances hit the floor as a result of that purchase. Well, now this insurance money has luckily given us another chance to make some smart moves, and I must demand that we do. We have to take another several steps in the right direction, or our money will surely suffer, and as a result, so will we. And I'm growing weary of the current regime. Life, I like what you said about the reasonably-priced car, and I think I'm willing to contribute to your cause. What can I do?"

Surprised, Life replied, "Well, we could contribute money to the local church, beyond that little token from the insurance money. That would be a great start."

"Oooh, well, you know," stammered Finance, "I've never been on board with that whole concept. Kind of throwing money away, in my opinion...."

Life sighed disappointedly.

"Good call, Finance," congratulated Pleasure.

"No, I really don't think I want to do that," continued Finance. "And I know that Mr. Chairman doesn't want that either. Which is exactly why I'll do it," he stated in nervous defiance.

"What?" questioned Pleasure, stunned and aggravated.

"What?" Life asked doubtfully.

"Yeah, I said I'll do it," said Finance. "I'll approve those funds to be given to the church. Not because I want to, but because everything we've done to this point has gone wrong. So I guess we've got to do the opposite. Something needs to change, and let's start with that."

"Wow," said Life. "That's great."

"Are you nuts, Finance?" asked Pleasure. "I won't 'okay' that at all. I see you defying me, and you will be repaid."

"Do your worst," said Finance, still nervous, but gaining confidence. "You've already messed me up bad enough with your poor stewardship. I'm not going to back your decisions anymore."

"Go ahead, join the losing side," said Pleasure haughtily. "But beware, by the end of this, you guys might find yourselves sitting on the *outside* of the boardroom."

"I am willing to take that chance to improve our condition," said Life, gaining momentum with Finance's spiel. "What do you think, Health?"

"You know I'm not satisfied either," said Health. "You all know what's going on in this body. We certainly aren't getting any healthier. Our diet stinks, and our exercise is tapering off. C'mon guys, we used to love basketball, and softball, and now what do we do? Get high and throw some darts? That's not healthy! Life, what does your new program have to say about health and fitness?"

"Well," replied Life, "it does stress the importance of taking care of the body. And of course, it greatly reduces alcohol and smoking."

"That's all you needed to say. I'm in," said Health.

"You silly simpletons," scoffed Pleasure. "So easily sweet-talked."

"They're entitled," responded Life. "What about you, Happiness?"

"I just know I'm not happy anymore," said Happiness sorrowfully. "I think your plan is to make me happy again. I was happy a long time ago, and I'm happy when I think about hope and God, so maybe there's some value to your plan. I'm with you."

"Great!" replied Life. "And how about you, Competition?"

"All I know is that we can kick these addictions' butts!" shouted Competition. "High-five? High-five?" He looked around holding his hand up. Health leaned over and gave him an uninspired hand-slap. "High-five!" hollered Competition, and he popped up and did a quick lap around the table, returning to his seat. "Sign me up, coach! Oh, yeah!" he said to Life. He wasn't known for his wisdom, but he certainly had boundless energy.

"You numbskull," mocked Pleasure under his breath.

"Hey, I will kick your butt if I have to," said Competition pointing directly at Pleasure, undaunted.

"Your ignorance is going to get you in trouble..." warned Pleasure.

"Glad to see your enthusiasm, Competition," said Life, trying to retain order. "We just have to find the right technique to beat these addictions. And the right course of action may just be God. Your thoughts, Conscience?"

"I have held from the start that something is wrong," began Conscience. "We've departed too far from the path we started on. On the original path was near-endless joy. On this path is a destructive sadness. We need to change paths. I continue my support for you, Life, and the work you are doing. Please, fix this problem, I beg you."

"I'll do all I can, my friends," replied Life, "but I need your help."

"Okay, we've heard enough out of you and your cronies," complained Pleasure. "You guys are treading on thin ice here. There is no 'strength in numbers' in this Committee. Let's look to a different source. What do you say, Society?"

"I'm all about the party life," began Society slyly. "It's a necessity to my continued development, as we found out in college. You know that the popular crowd vindicates drinking, and I also enjoy the power of a little rebellion with the pot. I mean, how many hundreds of times have we gone out partying? And the overall effect has been minimal. But look at all our friends. Look at how popular we are in this circle, and in our hometown. My vote is for no change at all. It doesn't take a genius to see that this God idea is not a popular one. You want to become one of those pathetic Bible-thumpers? No, you guys want to hang with me and Pleasure and the 'in' crowd."

"Well-put," vindicated Pleasure. "I admit, fellow members, that we've been on some wild rides together, but I have always seen us through, and I will continue to. This is the winner's side, as time has proven. Rejoin me now, and save yourself some agony. What is your standpoint on this topic, Logic?"

"Well," began Logic, "something does need to change here, Pleasure, that's for sure. But Life, I'm sorry that you've fallen into such foolishness. There are a million reasons that there isn't a God, as Society could tell you. I don't even have time to get into them all. First and foremost, no scientific evidence whatsoever. Where's the proof? Anything that I believe needs to have backing, and this theory has none. Don't you remember the craziness of those Bible stories? Have you ever seen a blind man given sight, simply by spoken word? Or a cripple walk, or a guy strutting across a lake on top of the water? Those are fairy tales, disconnected from reality. I've never seen or heard God. The Bible is an ancient book probably found in a cave somewhere, and you want to try to justify basing life on that? Certainly I've always loved to debate this topic, so I encourage you to try to convince me, but you're fighting a losing battle."

"Some very valid points," agreed Pleasure. "This new path you want to forge, Life, is usually in direct conflict with what I like, and what feels good. Not to mention, it's fantasy. I certainly won't condone such blatant foolishness."

"Well, for now I will continue to gather evidence," said Life, "but we do need to decide what we are going to do in the form of the change you mentioned, Logic. Now back in October I proposed that we consider moving away from this hometown, in the interest of change, since most of us agree that a change is necessary. I would also like to continue monetary support for Dad's church.

What do we have to give you, Pleasure, for you to agree to this deal?"

"Sorry, pal," said Society arrogantly. "We're not going anywhere. We've got a lot of friends here. We're not going to leave them. Tell him, Pleasure."

"So you want to throw away money to the church too, huh?" Pleasure asked Life. "That's going to cost a little extra."

"You're considering this?" demanded Society. "We can't move, you've always said we wouldn't move. You'd better be messing around, Pleasure."

"Or what?" returned Pleasure brashly. "Shut up for a minute, Society, and trust me, would you? Okay, Life, here's what you have to give me if you want your precious move. First, if we move out of this town, we move in with our best friend downstate, an hour from the girlfriend. Second, I get to do whatever I want with the rest of the insurance money. Third, I get to be in charge until the money is gone, and we don't have another meeting until the six-month meeting in June, no matter what."

"Great," muttered Finance.

"So, what do you think, Life?" asked Pleasure arrogantly. "Going to ante up on this one? Do you want your move and your 'God-money'?" He was sure Life would turn it down, and he exchanged knowing nods with Society.

After a lengthy dramatic pause, Life said, "Deal!"

"Are you kidding?" asked Society, outraged. "We're not moving! We're not! Take it back, Pleasure. If you don't take it back, I'm gonna... I'll have to..."

"You'll have to what?" asked Pleasure threateningly. "I'm not going to take it back. I get a ton of cash and free reign and no meetings. I can't believe you went for it, Life, you're dumber than I thought. Let's pack it in, we're moving downstate! Meeting adjourned!"

Pleasure excitedly left the boardroom. Some of the members shot Life questioning glances, while others gave him approving nods. But like Pleasure, Life also left the boardroom that day with a spring in his step.

chapter 7: **movement**

finally arrived at a conclusion in December of 2002. My current circle of friends was on a downward spiral, and I was riding along. It seemed that wherever I went in Alpena, my partying reputation preceded me. Some acquaintances would ask, "Hey man, what are you doing tonight? Let's go get trashed!" Others wanted to know where they could get some drugs, or where the big party was tonight. Everywhere I turned, I felt almost socially obligated to party, or plan to party, or know about partying. I couldn't get away from it.

At least I couldn't get away from it in my hometown. I decided that living at my grandma's was not far enough away from the pressing party crowd. I called up my best friend downstate, who was living with his girlfriend while she attended college. He talked with her and their other roommate, and they decided that they were willing to take on another roommate to help defray the cost of their townhouse. I knew my friend was still a partier, but I thought I could at least eliminate most of the Alpena-crowd influence by moving out of town. And besides, my best friend was one of the more "responsible partiers" who could still party and function responsibly, like me. And I knew his girlfriend and the other girl living there were serious about school, so I would have to tone down my irresponsibility. In a decision that shook the security of my life to the very core, I said farewell to my professional job and my party circle and moved four hours downstate to the "big city" of Lansing in January of 2003.

The move was fairly easy, as I really didn't have many possessions of value at the time. My friend had an extra bed, so I really only had to bring my clothes and my knick-knacks. My room was secluded in the basement, and my best friend and his girlfriend, and the other roommate, had bedrooms on the second floor. It was a well-kept complex, and a nice townhouse, though it was a little pricey. My insurance money went most of the way toward sponsoring my move, but I wasn't spending it wisely at all. I had no job lined up, but the first order of business was to celebrate. My best friend and I went to the bar almost every night during the first several weeks of my arrival, and I was spending cash like crazy. He had already set up a new circle of friends who were just as party-prone as my hometown group. So we all went out and got high, and got trashed, and I often sprung for the bill. After all, I could afford it, and I liked to pretend I was a "high-roller."

As my reckless partying continued, I was constantly facing the physical consequences of excessive alcohol and drug use. I would usually sleep past noon, but would still wake up feeling like crap from the night before. My insides felt lumpy and uncomfortable, until I was again "medicated" with alcohol or pot. My feet were often cold and clammy in the morning, and I had a hard time waking them up. And my throat continued to give me problems, often threatening to close right up after a heavy-smoking night. But during this phase of "celebration," I was facing a problem I had seen rarely in the past—memory loss.

Sure, in college, from time to time, I would get completely hammered at a friend's house, and forget a thing or two from the night before. Like the time I woke up in my townhouse bedroom with grass stains all over my clothes and had no idea how I had gotten there. Later, I would hear the story about how I had been dragged, singing and cursing, all the way from my friend's townhouse back to mine. And everybody got a good laugh. But my memory problems became a lot less funny when they started happening every night. Oftentimes, there would be a point that my memory just stopped recording, while my body was apparently on autopilot for the remainder of the evening. I was becoming more and more of a belligerent drunk, as my lack of happiness manifested itself in my "weakest moments." When I had no control of myself, the "true me" would emerge, and the "true me" wasn't a very nice guy at the time. I would wake up in the morning, and as far as my memory could tell, I had gone to bed early. But my body told me otherwise, displaying my typical symptoms of hangover. I would wait around with anticipation until my best friend got up, and I could get the run-down on everything I had done the night before. Often, we had gone to parties or bars I couldn't even remember. Sometimes I had even driven.

There was nothing more frightening to me about drinking and smoking than mental symptoms. When I started to lose pieces of who I was, my very own memories, I knew it was time to pull out all the stops on beating this consuming party-life. Many times I really and earnestly prayed that God would save me from this mental death. But the best I could do was cut back a little, trying to reduce the frequency of the memory loss. I couldn't stop myself from getting plastered once I started drinking, so I had to try to stop myself from drinking at all.

One morning, I woke up with one of my good female friends in my bed with me, and consequently, no memory of what had happened the night before. I did know that I had gotten wasted, or it seemed like I was heading that way during our cookout at about seven o'clock the previous night. But after that, I had no idea. I just knew my girlfriend wasn't going to like this much. A little while later I called my girlfriend, and being the moral guy I was, told her everything I knew. And as far as I knew, from what my memory told me, nothing had happened.

The move, the bar tabs, and other poorly-timed purchases had completely diminished all of my insurance money in just one month. It was again time to switch on my responsible side and find a job, and also try to stop the mental symptoms of my addictions. I went to an employment agency, and they had me hired in to another desk-job fairly quickly. This job was a little less professional than my previous one, but it financed my continued juggling of party and responsibility. With the addition of this obligation, I cut back on week-day partying, and my memoryless episodes were greatly reduced. I was far from the stigma of the town that had cultivated my irresponsibility. I was closer to my girlfriend, so I could visit her frequently. I lived with my best friend, so I hung out with him all the time. Once I had my job, things again looked to be settling down in a good way.

But things inside me were not settling down at all. I laid in my bedroom, in the basement of the townhouse, and I often cried. I kept up my financial support of my dad's church via mail, and I tried to pray and read the Bible a little, but nothing could touch my drinking and smoking problem. Most of the time, I concluded that it was impossible to beat. Which again made me cry. I didn't want to live this life, controlled by my habits instead of my heart. I felt like I was better than this, like I had more potential. But my failures indicated that I apparently did not.

I had made some substantial moves, trying to rid myself of the partying, but I still found myself a disaster internally. I was "cool" around the guys, or coworkers, or my girlfriend, but when I sat there all by myself, I was miserable. I was searching, but I wasn't finding anything except a harder life. All I could think of was that I needed to make some more movement. But what else could I do? As far as I could tell, change wasn't working, and neither was God. It seemed that all I could do was wait on life, helplessly tossed by its flow.

date: june 30, 2003
purpose: six-month review
agenda: status report, continued change

As life seemed to toss me around, I started to wonder if I really could do anything to combat the ups and downs of life. I just felt like everything I was doing had no bearing on where I was going. And I was going down. Still, my childhood, in which I had no control, was the happiest time of my life. So I determined that control wasn't necessary for happiness. In fact, most of the members of my control system, the Committee, didn't play a role in my youthful joy. Perhaps change had to start in the hierarchy of the Committee instead of the physical factors of my life.

I realized that I had essentially been living a double life. I had a public image, dictated in large part by Society, which most of the world saw. This image was a strong, independent young man, seeking to advance himself in the business world. He was quick-witted, optimistic, and happy. He was everything responsible about me. Too bad he was just a mask.

The "real me" was also independent; I wouldn't listen to anybody but myself. I wasn't happy, I wasn't optimistic, and I was starting to not even care about any sort of advancement in life. I was a slave to my addictions; they were becoming a big part of who the "real me" was. And nothing anybody could say would change my mind or convince me I was doing anything wrong. Once my public image was peeled back, the "real me" was quite a shady character, and I was starting to hate him. I was starting to hate myself. I just wished that the "real me" was a lot more loveable. I wanted my "secret identity" to be a hero, not a villain.

The Committee was a bustle of activity, ready for the end of the six months in which Pleasure had been playing dictator. The members could see more and more that he had no interest in their well-being, but they knew that their power against him was very limited.

Pleasure strutted into the boardroom. "Wow, that was a heck of a six months, wasn't it? I had the time of my life. Did you see that girl I woke up with? She was cute! I'll have to do that more often," he bragged.

"Yeah, real great," said Finance cynically. "$4,500 gone in the first month. You are one poor spender, my friend."

"Yeah, you've got us in quite a mess, physically and mentally," said Health.

"Now guys, let's chill out and remember who we're talking to," scolded Pleasure arrogantly. "Life made this deal, if you'll recall. Don't blame me if it turned out bad."

"Your lack of logic continues to amaze me," said Life. "Here we sit at the tail-end of your 'free roam', and all you can do is blame *me*? It doesn't matter, everyone here is starting to see the truth about you."

"Really?" asked Pleasure proudly, "And what is that truth?"

"That you are only here for you, not the rest of the Committee," answered Life. "But that's okay, I've always known it, Pleasure. I just wanted you to prove it to them."

"All your devious behavior will be for naught, Life," said Pleasure calmly. "Spread your political shenanigans, I don't care. I am the chairman, and it's only by my kindness that you even have a seat here."

"Life plays a role in this Committee," interjected Logic, "just like everyone else. You can't fault him for voicing his opinions, hair-brained as they may be. And we all agree that more change is necessary, that no one is really satisfied with the way things are going. You know I strongly object to the memory-loss issue."

"You guys and your change," said Pleasure, shaking his head. "I've got an idea for you. The girlfriend..."

"Yeah, *you* really care about the girlfriend," said Conscience judgmentally.

Pleasure shot him an evil glance. "Anyway," Pleasure continued, "the girlfriend's graduation is coming up pretty soon, and maybe she could come on over and live here for a while. That would be a nice change, adding a little more love into the mix, to cheer us up."

"I think we have different definitions of the word 'love'," said Life quietly.

"I think that would be a good idea, don't you guys?" asked Pleasure.

"Sounds good to me," said Society.

"How exactly is that going to work?" asked Finance doubtfully. "You know, from a financial standpoint?"

"How is it going to work from a *moral* standpoint?" asked Conscience.

"You guys are giving me a dang headache," griped Pleasure. "How about this: we'll see how it goes financially, and we can always get a second job if we have to, to make ends meet. Since I'm sure you guys won't let me go back to selling a bag here and there."

"On one condition," said Life. "If you let me have a little more time, say five minutes each day, to conduct more research into God by reading the Bible, then I guess we can live with the girlfriend with the option of the second job."

"Five minutes on weekdays only," countered Pleasure.

"Agreed," said Life.

"Finally!" said Pleasure, exhausted. "You guys are putting me through the dang ringer every meeting these days. What happened to those days of one-minute meetings?"

"I think we outgrew them," said Logic. "There are just too many factors out there to make snap-decisions."

"Hey Logic," started Life. "Do you want to know what I've discovered about God?"

"Sure," said Logic patronizingly. "What have you found out about the Big Fella?"

"He is said to teach by example," said Life. "He explains things in the simplest way so that there is no intelligence requirement for his help."

"That's great, Life," said Logic sarcastically. "Does he also zap people with lightning bolts? I've been waiting for mine."

"Gee, guys, I'd love to keep this up," said Pleasure, "but I've got better things to do. This meeting is adjourned."

chapter 8: **what's in store?**

After moving to Lansing, and the brief partying explosion, my life again entered a period of monotony. I was working my eight-to-five desk job, and afterward, sometimes my best friend and I would go work out or play basketball, and sometimes we would get high and just watch basketball on TV. I continued to entertain the notion of stopping the smoking and drinking, and started another long chain of failed quitting attempts. My best friend also bounced back and forth, sometimes laying off one or the other for a while. But neither of us could ever get away from it completely, as there always seemed to be an excuse to get drunk and high. Usually, getting out of work for the day was a good enough excuse.

Life continued this way into the summer of 2003 when my girlfriend graduated from college. Our relationship had some serious problems, most based on the fact that the majority of our ties to each other were pot and sex related. Did we love each other? That wasn't really even our question. We had decided we liked each other enough to be together, so we were together. When she got done with college, we tentatively decided that we liked each other enough to live together. It was like we shrugged our shoulders and asked "Why not?" Since I already had a job in Lansing, we decided it would be best if she moved over to where I was. I left my roommates in the townhouse, and my girlfriend and I got a quaint, garden-level, one-bedroom apartment together. Yet another change in my life, partially distracting me from the real problems.

Our apartment was in a nice neighborhood, so it wasn't cheap, even split two ways. She eventually got a job working in an art gallery, and we were doing "okay" financially. As far as partying, I managed to cut down my drinking almost completely to the weekends, and the pot-smoking was on-again, off-again. But my girlfriend and I definitely had some issues, so any time things would get rocky, we were back to getting high to patch things up. This pattern continued through the fall.

I wasn't used to someone in my life, "cramping my style" so much, and my partying was an escape from that. It was an escape from a lot of things. Sometimes she would ride me for my excessive use, especially on the weekend, so I often looked for ways to evade her heckling. That, coupled with our financial concerns, led me to seek a second job. My best friend had been working at a liquor store for a while, and I asked if he could get me in as a stock boy. That fall, I found myself stocking shelves at the liquor store every Thursday and Saturday night.

This job seemed like a perfect solution. Unlike my "semi-professional" day job, I could actually get high and drunk while working at the liquor store. It didn't take a lick of brainpower, and it got me away from my "buzz-killer" girlfriend. Most of the time I could just stand around, talking with my coworkers or leafing through the nudie-magazines. Occasionally, I would have to go back to the cooler and restock some beer or haul a keg out to someone's car, but for the most part I could relax.

The cooler was a stock boy's sanctuary. I would go back to the cooler and smoke pot sometimes, and if I wanted beer, every possible brand surrounded me. Nobody really kept tabs on exact beer counts, so snagging a bottle or six here and there was no problem. I would get high, or do some drinking, and then go out and wander the aisles of the store, making sure the shelves were properly stocked. After my shift, I would pop in some minty gum and head home to my girlfriend. My paycheck usually became my "party budget," so she wasn't giving me flack for taking out of our general funds for my bad habits.

I spent a lot of time at that party store. It was well maintained, as far as liquor stores go, but was well on its way to becoming run-down. It seemed that people didn't need an aesthetically pleasing place to buy liquor. The store was situated on a strip in a decent neighborhood, concealing the ugliness of the trailer park hidden directly behind it. Like any liquor store in a college town, we had a lot of young customers, buying tons of cases and kegs for their parties. We also had distinguished customers, who often knew the owner, and bought our finest liquors and wines. And we had customers who were known as "the regulars."

The college partiers didn't surprise me at all. I had seen and partied with thousands of their type. The higher-classers I had dealt with in my "professional" job, and they seemed to be quite prevalent throughout society as well. But the regulars astonished me. They were a new breed of people whose existence I had not acknowledged prior to my liquor store job. I knew poverty was out there, hiding behind the public face, but for the first time, I saw poverty in human form.

The various regulars would come in throughout the night, and the employees would often strive to strike up conversations to break the monotony. Usually, the regulars were nice people who had a problem. And usually that problem was what they had come to purchase. They continued to choose alcohol, and by default were also choosing a life of deficiency. Some of them had no clue what was happening around them. But they each brought a unique contribution to the flavor of the party store.

"Ghost Lady" freaked me out because she had such a zombie appearance. She would wander through the store, staring straight ahead, mumbling, her wiry white hair in every direction. The pupils of her eyes were almost as white as her hair—completely empty. I had nightmares about her occasionally. She was a shadow of a human; a slave to alcohol and whatever other drugs were controlling her life. I wondered how she let it get that bad.

"Forty" couldn't remember a thing from day to day. He was a nice guy, tall and wiry, sporting the classic greasy mullet-and-cap combo. There was no chance he would ever remember a name or a detail you told him. He just came in and bought the same malt liquor over and over again. He consistently called one of my coworkers by the wrong name, and the one time he was corrected, he slunk out of the store embarrassed. He returned the next day, calling him by the same incorrect name. I supposed I could identify with his forgetfulness.

"Natty Ice" was a nice guy, again, always buying the exact same beer every night. He was a thicker man, also sporting a nice long mullet. We talked with him about his life, and he was a very personable fellow. Later, we heard that he had assaulted and nearly killed a friend with a baseball bat. That seemed out of character, and I had to consider that maybe the "nice guy" was hiding something deeper that wasn't so nice. I could kind of relate, since the "real me" also had some secret anguish.

One of the regulars was a very tall, very nice man, probably about forty-five years old, who lived in the trailer closest to the store. He was guaranteed to be at the store at least three times in a six-hour shift. He was full of great stories, though they were usually amazingly embellished, and he told some hilarious jokes. He was also full of liquor. He often helped out around the store, usually requesting payment in the form of some Jack Daniels shooters. I got to be good friends with this man, and sometimes I would go over to his trailer on break to smoke a bowl and watch TV with him.

This man often told stories of his high school days, when he was a star athlete who even held some records in track. He also told of his twin brother, who apparently had risen to a more prominent position in life than this story-teller. This "regular" seemed to have had everything going for him at one point in his life. In fact, the twin was proof that he could have been successful. But instead, he lived in a beat-up trailer, doing chores for liquor.

Many regulars had similar lives and stories, but there was usually a common thread. That thread was alcohol, or other various drugs, that had taken them down their impoverished paths, and essentially left them with an "addiction" for a personality. I couldn't judge these people though, because I was tempting the same destructive path. It was as if I was at a fork in the road of life and had been treading water since my Christmas discovery, given the option of success or failure. Until I worked at that liquor store, I had never seen such poignant examples of how choosing failure could result. A human being who is a ghost of his potential was so much more penetrating than the "druggie brochure" a coworker had once given me. The brochure had told me that if I did drugs, I might end up in the gutter. It even had a cute little illustration. But until that illustration manifested in my reality, in the form of the "regulars," I didn't catch on. Alcohol wasn't going to leave any of these people's lives until they were dead, and it wasn't going to leave me either. It was my responsibility to leave alcohol.

As I realized more and more about the destructive power of my addictions, I began to petition God more. Sometimes I forgot his existence was in question for me, and just cried out, knowing full-well that I needed help from some source. "Please, help me, God! Help me anyone! Do whatever you have to, just help me!" I just couldn't let myself end up like those regulars, it didn't matter how nice they seemed. I knew that eventually I could be there if I didn't cut those habits out of my life completely. I also knew that I couldn't win the fight alone.

date: december 15, 2003
purpose: twelve-month review
agenda: status reports, upcoming year change
       and planning

I thought I had a pretty well-rounded Committee with my nine members. I thought for the most part, that I was considering every angle when making my decisions. Pleasure led my decision-making, accepting limited amounts of council from the other eight members: Competition, Conscience, Finance, Happiness, Health, Life, Logic, and Society. I thought I had a pretty good handle on living.

I had figured out that my existence, most simply broken down, was a scale on which I lived. On one end of this scale was "good" and at the other was "bad." Each and every day of life, I fell somewhere on that scale; I felt good, or I felt bad, or I felt somewhere between. And the Committee members worked in the same manner. Each of them represented a different scale within my life. In other words, each member could bring to the Committee a report of "good" or "bad," or any rating in between. So if, for example, I got a great job, Finance might report that all things were "good" in his area. On a downturn, Finance would report "bad," and possibly suggest a plan for change. If things were stable, there would be an "okay" rating, and Finance would probably not speak up. Each of the members operated on a similar scale in their respective areas.

I essentially had nine "well-being meters" that reported to me how good or bad life was from their perspective. If one or more slipped below "okay," a change was required, and the Committee would deliberate on that change at their next meeting. The fact that many of my Committee members had been discontent regarding the partying made for frequent issues. Though Pleasure usually had a "good" report, through the help of my habits, the other members often weren't seeing things so rosy.

During the period when I was working at the party store, life calmed way down. Though I still had my fair share of struggles, including the ongoing attempts to quit drinking and pot-smoking, I had a lot of time to reflect on my life. An anticlimactic period was probably what I needed, after the crash and the move. It was during this time that I thought about all that had happened in my life to that point. I did a lot of contemplating on the accident, and how the insurance money had facilitated my move downstate. So the question came to my mind, was rolling my Expedition a good or a bad thing?

Of course, as I was flying through that ditch at 65 miles-per-hour, my first inclination was to write it off as bad. Pleasure didn't like what was going on at all. And of course, each of the other members saw some sort of threat to their existence, so their primary response was also negative. But then I survived. Then I got the insurance money. Then I was able to move, and now I was cutting back little-by-little on partying. It seemed to me that perhaps that accident was a *good* thing—just what I needed to surpass a trouble-spot in my life. This line of reasoning is what gave birth to the tenth member of the Committee: the Greater Good.

Each of the members had their little scale that would rate my condition in their area, but no one was looking at the big picture, especially not Pleasure. He was determining most everything about my life, trying to throw the other members a placating bone when they drooped below "okay" on the scale and started complaining. Under Pleasure's leadership, my life was essentially one-dimensional. But I had to start considering the good of all the members collectively, and the possibility of elevating each of their scales beyond the stick-point at "okay." The accident, which was not a pleasurable experience, had ultimately helped me out, and could now be rated as "good" overall. In the same way, Greater Good looked at the well-being of each member, evaluating all factors to produce a solution that may be temporarily bad for some, but would ultimately elevate the well-being of each member and the sum of the members: me.

"Well, I guess it is my 'pleasure' to introduce a new member to the Committee," started Pleasure, annoyed. "As if we need more members. But anyway, this is 'Greater Good.' Why don't you stand and tell us a little bit about yourself? Oh, and why you're here."

"Thank you," said Greater Good with a respectful smile. He was an older man, probably seventy, who looked like he had lived a rough life, but had still come through it with dignity and optimism. He was bald, and had a short white beard covering his weathered skin. He wore a white dress shirt and black pants. "I'm not here to make a big stir," he began. "I recently had a lengthy conversation with Logic, and he mentioned that things on the Committee were not going so well. I had a few ideas that I thought maybe could help, so Logic invited me along."

"Thanks for that, Logic," said Pleasure sarcastically. "Anyway, the Committee is fine. We're just going through a hard phase, that's all. We'll come through it soon."

"And what evidence of that claim do we have?" asked Logic.

"My word should be evidence enough," retorted Pleasure angrily. "You rabble-rousers still don't understand what kind of power I have, do you?"

"I don't want to create problems," said Greater Good humbly. "I just wanted to silently observe; maybe give a thought here or there."

"What kind of thoughts do you have?" asked Health, testing him.

"Well," started Greater Good, "an idea you might like is for future physical well-being. Has anyone here considered how much the human body can truly take as far as poor diet and exercise regimens? Where will continued neglect leave us in ten years, or twenty? Has anybody made the connection that when Health hurts now, it is only a matter of time before Competition and Pleasure and Happiness suffer as well? Being out of shape reduces the ability to compete, and can eventually diminish overall condition of life. Sure, the effects aren't noticeable overnight, but I specialize in the long-term, and I guarantee that they will catch up. So that means we have to be conscientious about them now."

"I knew that," lied Pleasure.

"I like this guy," said Health, satisfied. "Welcome aboard."

"Thank you," said Greater Good.

"Do me," said Finance. "Talk about my future."

"Well, your future is somewhat similar to Health's," said Greater Good. "Pleasure, and Happiness, and Logic have some aspirations for the future: a house, maybe a family, some nice vacations. But you're a part of that too. Without some level of continued financial prudence, those things can never be theirs."

Competition stood up and pointed. "This guy kicks butt!" he shouted.

"Oh, please," said Pleasure. "You're a good politician, but what is your plan, Greater Good? How are we going to make these things happen?"

"All we have to do is live a little more responsibly each day," answered Greater Good. "Improvement is all we need to do."

"Why didn't I think of that?" mocked Pleasure. Despite the chairman's pessimism, most of the other members showed instant support for Greater Good.

"I think he's got some good ideas," said Logic. "Of course, we part ways on a few topics, but I think his ideas are a worthy addition to the Committee."

"What topics do you disagree on?" wondered Life.

"Well," started Logic, "his plans that consider the long-term are great; the way they combine all of the things we want into an attainable bundle really motivates me. But he also suggests being a bit *too* helpful to the less fortunate. Why on earth should I go and help someone rake their yard or move their belongings? There is no logical benefit to us."

"I just want you to understand that existence is a lot bigger than just 'us'," replied Greater Good. "Sometimes we have to do unpleasant things, putting personal well-being on hold."

"See, I just don't buy into that," said Logic. "I need to be able to see the benefit to me—cause and effect—before I can get on board with a program."

"My contention is that you need to get on board *before* you can see the benefit," replied Greater Good. "Some situations do not have a painless solution."

"I agree entirely," responded Logic. "But it is completely illogical that all of the members should suffer; some can sacrifice a little, so the others can increase a lot. But if we all sacrifice a lot, we aren't accomplishing anything positive."

Most of the other members agreed with Logic—that they would have to understand a plan and how it would better serve them individually and entirely before they would go along with it. But there was something about Greater Good's plans that secretly intrigued the Committee as well. Even Pleasure was curious as to his methods.

"You guys just don't understand... the 'big picture' is a lot bigger...." trailed off Greater Good, but he was having a little trouble getting his point across. Though the members liked his strategies, he still didn't fit in well with the group. The other members still had selfish outlooks, but he brought a refreshingly considerate viewpoint which alienated him.

"I'm afraid it's going to be a while until this guy fits in," Life said to himself.

"Anyway," said Pleasure, "speaking of the future, let's talk New Year's celebration."

"I think the New Year is a great time to quit the partying once and for all," said Life.

"That's great," said Pleasure sarcastically. "You go right ahead and quit."

"I'm serious," said Life.

"So am I," said Pleasure deviantly. "I give you full permission to quit. Go right ahead. In fact, let's have one last celebration, you know, to emphasize the quitting. One more party, and then we can be done."

"Fine," said Life. "It's not a great idea, but I guess we can allow one more time."

"As if you had a choice," said Pleasure arrogantly. "Meeting adjourned."

chapter 9: "last hurrah"

In December of 2003, I was again getting fed up with how my life was going. Sure, I managed to keep a couple of jobs, but I definitely was not happy, or healthy, or financially sound. I wanted something different. My girlfriend also agreed that there was something amiss, and that likely, quitting smoking pot and drinking would go a long way to solving whatever it was. So we decided that we were going to give up pot for the New Year. I thought maybe I'd have a shot if we did it together. Of course, we wanted to go out with a bang, so we planned our "last hurrah." We were going to make some pot brownies, like we had on occasion before, but this time we were going to make them really potent. Our plan was to eat them on New Year's Eve and have one last good old time, just me and her, before we completely gave up the party life. Maybe if we made an event of it, quitting would be easier. Sounded great in theory.

About a week before New Year's, I came down with some kind of sickness that left me in bed for about three days. I was as bedridden as I'd ever been since I was a child. I had to call in sick for an actual sickness, not the "morning-after syndrome," and because I had been so irresponsible with my sick days, I had to use vacation time. Being so weak and ill made me start to question if I was going to be able to get better for our New Year plan. Eventually, I started to buck up a little. Though my better judgment told me that with a weakened immune system, I should not do the pot-brownie thing, I again decided against better judgment.

New Year's Eve rolled around and we made our brownies. This time we used really high-quality weed, and put in more pot than we ever had before. We ate them early in the evening and waited for the buzz to kick in. It started kicking a half-hour later, and then a half-hour after that it started kicking the crap out of us. I had never been so high, which was all well and good, until my girlfriend started to feel sick to her stomach.

Sitting on our ugly yellow couch, she started throwing up the brownies, and I took her outside to get some fresh air. Neither of us had ever puked from weed before, and even the dabbling we'd done with "shrooms" hadn't given us this intense of a high. I knew my girlfriend was freaking out hard since she had vomited, and I was getting pretty paranoid myself. The pot coursed through my veins, and I could barely think straight. I tried to focus on calming her down, though I was getting pretty worried about the both of us. I knew I had to hold it together, for her and for us. We walked around the apartment building several times, hoping to knock down our highness, but had no success; it just kept growing. At one point, I almost puked, but I focused all I could on holding it together so we could get through this. We went inside, then outside, then inside again.

Nothing was working. We both got really tired, and she wanted to just pass out, but I didn't think that was such a good idea if she was getting sick. So we clung to our consciousness, and went back outside. She sat hunched over on our back step, and I sat next to her trying to console her and tell her she was alright, though I had no idea. And I told her that she knew the consequences, and I knew the consequences, but if she wanted me to call an ambulance I would. I certainly couldn't depend on my own judgment at that point. She considered it, and then began to have trouble breathing. She gave me the nod, and I went inside and called for an ambulance. I quickly ran back to the step to make sure she was still conscious.

The cops responded quickly. I didn't waste one second trying to throw out my weed, but instead stayed by her side until they arrived. When they got there, we immediately began to feel calmness, that everything would be okay, as far as our lives and health. As far as our police records, I knew that was a different story. The ambulance arrived, and as the paramedics attended to my girlfriend, I could see the paranoia leave her. She realized the gravity of the situation, calling the cops on ourselves, and whispered to me that she was sorry. I told her it was okay. Then I went into our apartment, which was now crawling with cops.

The cops didn't treat me with much respect, though maybe I didn't deserve it. I was asked many questions as I cooperated completely in turning over my brownies and bag and pipes to them. They asked about my jobs and my life and my girlfriend. Answering all of those questions high was a lot easier than I thought because by that point, I just didn't care. I was in trouble, I knew. There was no need to hide my intoxication any more, because the worst thing that could happen to me had already happened. I actually had a good time talking with them, once I knew my girlfriend was alright.

They took all my paraphernalia, and finished putting me through the gamut as far as questions. To their credit, they did allow me to ride in the ambulance with my girl-friend, instead of taking me to jail to sober up. I hopped in the cab of the ambulance and had an enjoyable conversation with the driver, still completely high. He told me he never understood why people smoked pot, and I gave him the default response: "Because it was fun." We rode to the emergency room where the doctors did whatever they did to help her, and I sat and watched. I began to imagine what kind of trouble I was in, as thoughts bounced around my still-buzzing brain.

Sitting in the emergency room with my girlfriend in a hospital bed, I heard the "Happy New Year" announcement over the hospital speaker system. I had almost forgotten what day it was. Could "turning over a new leaf" get any more symbolic? I was continuously surprised at how calm I felt now that I was essentially "exposed" as a druggie. I had no way to hide it from society anymore.

I did a lot of thinking that night, most of which I don't remember. My mind jumped from one idea to the next as my high stayed strong until the sun came up. It was a killer buzz, but it had a pretty hefty price tag. I wondered what would become of me—if I would lose my job or never be able to work at another professional organization again. At least I had the liquor store job to fall back on.

That morning, we took a taxi back to our apartment from the hospital, both of us still high. Our wild night had finally ended, though we knew the consequences were going to have a future impact. We finally got to bed at about seven in the morning, but I couldn't sleep. I was thinking about God. Certainly if he was trying to send devastating life events my way, this was one of them. It even came with a built-in warning, with the sickness just days before. Was I being stupid if I couldn't see the symbolism and depth of this event? But it still didn't make logical sense to me.

I also had to ask myself why I did not seek other means for logically fixing the situation. Certainly, my buzz had left me with some limited mental capabilities, but why had I been such a fool as to not flush my pot before the cops came? Or disappear when I saw them coming, so my girlfriend could be helped and I could watch from a distance? Or just let her pass out? I had a lot of questions and not a lot of answers. All I knew for certain was that she was okay, and we were both in trouble.

date: january 1, 2003
purpose: emergency meeting
agenda: the new year's bust

Pleasure had masterminded the pot-brownie idea, and after that New Year's Eve unfolded, the Committee predictably went into an uproar. Finance wanted to tear Pleasure apart on account of the employment-related implications of a police record, and Happiness was at an all-time low. Conscience had some obvious "I-told-you-so's," and Life was not particularly amused either. The Committee met that New Year's Day when the effects of the pot wore off.

"I know I messed up," started Pleasure. "I'm sorry about that, but we just have to move forward from this point. Forget it even happened."

"Forget it even happened? Are you crazy?" ranted Finance. "Do you have any idea how this threatens our financial well-being for the rest of our lives? We might lose our job, and how are we going to get another with a police record? You've ruined everything, Pleasure!"

"Calm down, calm down," said Pleasure. "We're going to be fine."

"Sure, we'll live, but it's the quality of that life I'm worried about," retorted Finance sharply.

"I agree with Pleasure that we just need to move forward, though we can't ever forget this happened," said Greater Good.

"Yeah, see, just move ahead," agreed Pleasure. "We just need to determine what we're going to do about this situation." The members did a little muttering and whispering, but eventually agreed.

"My vote is for Life's plan," said Finance. "I'm ready to go full-bore into his whole 'God program'." Life's plan had bolstered a lot of support, though many of the members had yet to understand it. More specifically, most of the members desired change, and each change administered by Pleasure seemed to be making matters worse.

"Are you a fool?" asked Logic condescendingly. "We haven't even heard much of what this plan would actually call for. Plus God still makes no logical sense."

"I'll tell you what the plan would call for," said Life. "Following God's plan means that a whole lot of the things we currently do in this life need to be eliminated, and first on that list are alcohol and pot."

"We all know that, Life," answered Logic. "That's what we've been failing at for years now. How do you propose we do it?"

"Well," began Life, "we have let these drugs become a part of our life, a part of who we are. And when we don't have that part, we feel empty. So we fail over and over because that void sits empty until we get drunk or high again. What we need to do is start filling that void with positive things. If it sits empty, we will be right back into our old habits. But positive influence can help us compensate for that void. And a big part of that positive is God."

"I like the sound of that," said Happiness quietly. "How do we get this positive influence?"

"It's available everywhere, but we have to make an effort to seek it out," responded Life. "There are books, some in our bookcase right now, like the ones from Mom and Dad, that have positive messages for us, the first being the Bible, and many other simpler variations. We're already inspiring positivity by Finance's choice to give money to Dad's church. I suggest we also look into finding a church of our own down here."

"No, that's just silly," objected Society. "What is your goal, to become one of these crazy Bible-thumpers like Dad? Are we going to start preaching on street corners?

The financial contributions are crazy enough, and I don't see 'God' doing much for us right now, despite over a year's worth of payments to him."

"Are you sure?" asked Life. "I think God just showed up in a big way at our New Year's celebration."

"God?" asked Logic. "We make a slight miscalculation on the potency of the pot, and you see God at work? Are you still high?"

"Logic, I believe you overestimate your intelligence," said Life. "You remember the magician we were watching on TV the other night, right? Well, you couldn't keep up with some of his 'mind-reading' card tricks. He was doing some pretty amazing things that none of us understood. At the same time, we all agree that there had to be a logical explanation for the tricks. And you are essentially asking God to do the same thing—show you some impressive parlor tricks. So are you going to follow the next person who shows you a trick you can't understand? That doesn't seem logical. Or are you going to be cynical, just like when it comes to magic? My belief is that if you maintain your cynicism about God now, you would be just as cynical no matter what God showed you in the line of 'signs.' Plus you would be missing the point of what God is trying to do here."

"Maybe you're right, about the cynicism," agreed Logic, "but tell me, what is God trying to do?"

"He's trying to build up our human intangibles—love, faith, and hope—among others. Specifically, when we are asked to believe something we can't see, he is building our faith."

"Faith, huh?" asked Logic.

"Yes, faith," answered Life. "Remember back in elementary school when we were learning mathematics?"

"Fondly," said Logic. "What does that have to do with anything?"

"Well, learning takes two steps, like faith," said Life. "The first step is to grasp the concept, for example, of multiplication. It's easy to walk through the problem hand-in-hand with the teacher. But the real test comes with the second step, application, which is also where the real progress is made. A student learns by struggling. If he has no faith in what he has been taught, he will give up or do the problem wrong. At that point, he might call on the teacher, which may help him to learn a little, but shows he doesn't have confidence in his own ability to apply the principles of the instructor. Or he can struggle through the problem, holding tightly with confidence to the techniques the teacher has taught. Failure, postponement, and success are all options, but which one shows evidence of faith in both his ability and the teachings?"

"I suppose the third option, struggling through it, and succeeding," replied Logic.

"And that's what God wants from us," Life continued. "He wants us to have enough faith in his plan that we do not need him showing up all the time, holding our pencil as we write. He wants us instead to know his ways and have faith in what he has already shown us. Somewhere, deep down, we know what is right and wrong. Sure, he's willing to give hints, like perhaps a special New Year's message, but he likely won't show up to give us a physical spanking. And as we struggle, we learn to succeed."

"I see your point," said Logic, "that God is trying to teach us, but subtly, so we have to contribute effort of our own. Pretty shaky reasoning as far as I'm concerned; I think you're reading a little bit too deep into 'chance.' And we have yet to even address such things as Creation and Heaven, which is where the real scientific evidence comes into play."

"Oh, I'm sure we'll eventually discuss it all," said Life. "But for now, let *me* ask *you* a question."

"Okay, shoot," said Logic, gearing up for a chance to show his intelligence.

"When the girlfriend was getting sick, and eventually requested an ambulance, why didn't we dispose of our pot, or try anything to get off the hook for this drug charge? Why did we stay by her side instead of fending for ourselves and looking out for our well-being? That wasn't very logical at all."

"You're right, Life," admitted Logic. "Can I blame it on being high?"

"We both know it is deeper than that," said Life.

"I know," started Logic. "I guess it's because we care for her, because Pleasure and Happiness are both somewhat tied to her. Greater Good also insisted on putting her first. I guess they overruled me on this call. We wanted to make sure she was okay, first and foremost, before our own well-being. I knew it was going to be a sacrifice, but we decided to make it."

Greater Good spoke up. "So perhaps now you can see the reasoning behind my desire to help others. The greater good is not always the best possible outcome for the sum of this single human's elements. The greater good is often the best outcome for the sum of many humans combined. Existence is a whole lot bigger than just this Committee."

In contemplating my New Year's experience, I realized that my life had a lot more to do with the other people than I thought. I lived selfishly, like a child, forgetting to consider others in my "big equation." I was so consumed with my pathway through life that I failed to understand how much my course affects the courses of others. I had an opportunity to be a positive or negative influence on those around me. I wanted to be positive, but the problem was that sometimes making a positive contribution required sacrifice. And that was what Greater Good was trying to tell the Committee. That is what Greater Good was trying to show them when he insisted on helping my girlfriend first. Greater Good was about more than just my Committee.

"Bigger than this Committee, hey?" asked Logic curiously. "Well-spoken; let me give this some thought."

Each of the members agreed that they had had enough for now, and that they would again have to play the waiting game to see exactly what kind of legal trouble was on the way before we made any movements. Life had gained more support yet for his "God program," and even Pleasure seemed agreeable to giving a little more time for reading various positive books at the apartment.

"Meeting adjourned," said Pleasure.

chapter 10: **depression**

The 2004 New Year's bust left quite a mark on me. I knew my life was about to get harder as I waited for some sort of contact telling me what kind of trouble I was in. The theme of my life seemed to be failure. My semi-professional job was not going well; my poor attendance and lack of enthusiasm had put me in a probationary state, with six months to get my act together. I certainly had been a failure when it came to beating my addictions. My finances were "okay" at best, and I was a lazy, unmotivated druggie. The only silver lining was my girlfriend. Sure, our relationship had been on a decline to that point, but I was convinced that such a grandiose finale to our partying lives would bring us closer as we battled through sobriety together.

It turned out that my girlfriend and I didn't have a whole lot in common when pot was subtracted from our equation. Even our physical connection dwindled when the pot was gone. Most of the time we had nothing to do; either I was humoring her "artsy" activities or she was humoring my competitive ones. So a couple weeks after our New Year's fiasco, we decided on a trial breakup. She moved away to her friend's house hundreds of miles north, and I was left alone with my problems as our relationship hung in the balance. At first, I became very sad, and I really wanted her back. I felt like my heart was breaking, and I couldn't live without her. I told her that this solitude just wasn't working for me and that I wanted her to return. But she had other plans, and was easily distracted by the fun of living with her friend. She would not come back to me. I quickly realized that our breakup was more than just "trial."

Once my hope for our relationship was dashed, I no longer had anyone to turn to. Fortunately, unlike my girlfriend, the habits I had booted less than a month ago were more than willing to return to me. I again began to medicate myself heavily with my addictions, but this time I was typically alone. I shut out society as I sat in my little shell of alcohol and weed. My life was disappearing before my eyes. Night after night, I would accomplish nothing, progress nowhere. I could still motivate myself to go to work and put on the "responsible mask," because my habits needed an income. But beyond that, I became a shell of a human.

In the midst of my dismal depression, a new idea began to permeate my mind. I was a failure, that was undeniable, and I started to think I might be one forever. When presented with that possibility, and its increasing probability, I didn't want to live anymore. I sat in my small apartment alone, crying about my life and how it was unraveling. What did I have to live for? Failure after failure? I couldn't turn to my family, or my friends, because I would look like a fool. I had to continue to broadcast my strong, independent image, while my insides rotted. Again, I cried out to God, this time with an ultimatum. "If you don't do something to save me, I'm done with this life!" I threatened. "If I mean anything to you, you'd better show up in a big way! I can't fight off death much longer!" How could he sit idly by, if he existed, watching me suffer? But there was no answer, and thoughts of suicide continued to harass me.

Sometimes, I'd be standing in the kitchen making dinner, and I would get the urge to violently plunge a knife into my chest. Or I'd be driving, and I'd feel the insatiable desire to jerk the wheel into a semi. Just end it all, find out once and for all if God truly was out there. Death seemed better than the depression I was facing.

Eventually, I tried some reading in an attempt to make a slight positive contribution to my life. It took me a while, but I finished one of the books my dad had bought me. It was a book on fasting with some decent religious ideas, and some far-fetched ones. It basically said you could kind of get God's attention, let him know you were serious, if you made a decision to skip meals, sort of as a symbol of discipline. It sounded crazy to me, but what did I have to lose? So occasionally I would skip a meal here or there, trying to maybe get God to act in my life. A lot of the time, I didn't feel like eating anyway.

I talked about the fasting with my dad on the phone, and as part of my deceptive projection of how decent my life was, I announced to him I read through the book and was trying its concepts. He thought that was great, and he also mentioned that the author happened to be a pastor at a church in my city. He told me the name, and as was my tendency, I rushed my dad off the phone so I could get drunk and high.

Shortly after that conversation, while I was cruising the Internet at work, out of curiosity I looked this church up. In the picture, the building looked huge, like a sports stadium. "Maybe I'll give it a try sometime," I thought. I continued with my daily routine of a fairly responsible day at work, followed by the depths of depression at night. I began to get really anxious about the aftermath of the New Year's episode. It had been over two months, and I knew they would contact me soon. However, I didn't let anything stand in the way of my solitary drunkenness or pot smoking. My depression continued to hold me down, weakening me every day. It seemed apparent that God wasn't going to show up.

date: march 15, 2004
purpose: three-month review
agenda: status reports, depression

All things considered, life was going pretty crappy for me. I thought I knew what sadness was before, but Happiness was dwindling to new lows in the light of the breakup, my incompatibility with my job, and the unknown future likely containing drug allegations. I was ready to turn to anyone, or anything, that would help me.

Each of the members of the Committee was primed to follow Life's suggestion to seek out God except for Society, Logic, and of course Pleasure. No one knew if Pleasure would ever turn, and Logic was also a tough cookie to crack. But Society was a little more pliable, a little more open to change, under the depressing circumstances of my life. Logic was becoming a little concerned about how close the Committee was to making some very illogical decisions, under the influence of Life and Greater Good.

"Okay, Life, let's have it out," demanded Logic, before the meeting even began. "Sure, we need a change, but if control of the Committee is handed over to you, we'll probably be in just as much trouble as we are in now. Especially with Greater Good's schemes to 'save the planet,' that you seem to be buying into."

"Logic, you just can't think outside the box," responded Life. "There's so much below the surface in this existence; so much more that cannot be 'logically' explained. If you look at a human being, all you can see is flesh and blood, but how many thoughts and feelings and secret intricacies does that human have beneath the outer appearance? The majority of life is not in the physical world, yet that is where humankind puts most of its belief. Science cannot explain everything, especially when it comes to human emotion and behavior."

"You sure you want to bring science into this?" asked Logic. "Science will beat your 'magic' into oblivion. First and foremost, there is obviously no scientific proof that God exists."

"And none that he doesn't," countered Life, "or the controversy would be over. Science agrees completely with God; it is only man-made scientific *theory* that does not. Plus it is Biblical that he will not reveal himself for the sake of proving his existence. Belief is the key."

"That's convenient," said Logic cynically. "For the record, the Bible is inadmissible as a form of evidence. It's a couple-thousand-year-old storybook, and anyone who would base their life on at-best a semi-historical piece is not thinking logically."

"I don't expect you to put any trust in the Bible... yet," replied Life. "For the sake of this debate, I won't present it as fact. But we can agree that if nothing else, it has some good moral value to it, can't we?"

"Sure, I suppose it's noble to give, or to die for the sake of others," admitted Logic. "That's why I'm fine with a little Bible reading here and there. I won't deny that it's an interesting book."

"And I won't deny that it's hard to believe—the Bible, or God's existence," said Life. "But the reason God's existence is hard to believe is again because it is a test of faith. 'Good' cannot exist without a sliding scale, and at the other end of that scale is 'bad.' Happiness cannot exist without sadness. And faith cannot exist without doubt. The scale cannot exist without balance, positive on one side and negative on the other. It is our privilege to choose where we are going to spend most of our time on that scale."

"Okay, that's a neat little philosophy, but what's your point?" asked Logic.

"The point is that there is meant to be a lot of doubt; it is part of the design of our existence, so that there can be potential for great faith," replied Life. "All of the negative in the world is evidence for the potential of the positive."

"So you said 'it is our privilege to choose'," said Logic. "What do you mean by that?"

"I mean that our choices open up either positive or negative for ourselves, and others," answered Life. "The more positive we are subjected to, the better we will understand the positive and be able to project it into other lives. And often, we can *choose* to subject ourselves to certain positives. God is the biggest of these positives."

"So how do we subject ourselves to God?" asked Logic, doubtfully playing along.

"Prayer and Bible reading are two sources, but what a 'beginner' really needs is the influence of other more-developed believers," answered Life.

"Oh, so that's where you're going with this," responded Logic. "You want to go to church."

"Yeah, I do, and if you're okay with a little Bible reading, why not a little church too?" reasoned Life.

"Church is for the crazies," interjected Society, "I don't want to waste my time on that bunch of yahoos."

"Calm down, Society," said Logic. "It's also true that a lot of prominent figures go to church, and aren't too seemingly 'uncool.' I can consider it as an option."

"Come on, Logic!" retorted Society. "You can't be serious. Churches are filled with hypocrites and con artists, or people that are just plain nuts."

"No person is perfect, and neither is any organization," responded Greater Good. "To expect perfection is illogical. You act like there isn't one genuine person out there. To condemn humankind is to condemn yourself. This Committee has some major problems; that is clear. But there is hope here, I know it, just like there's hope for humankind as well. We just have to find it."

"Yeah, let's try to find it," urged Life. "And let's try the church."

"Inspiring," said Logic sarcastically. "I suppose as a test we can give church a try, sometime in the future. But we're kind of getting away from the debate on God's existence. I'm not going to sell out based on some emotional high; I need to have facts."

"Yes, facts are the basis of science, aren't they?" began Life. "In fact, essentially the goal of science is to collect facts and understand how they apply to our existence. Would I be correct to say so?"

"Sure," answered Logic.

"So the ultimate goal would be to understand everything about our existence, correct?"

"Yes."

"And once we understood everything about our existence—every disease cure, every machine malfunction, every mental disorder and its solution—we could essentially create for ourselves a perfect world, correct?" asked Life.

"In theory, I suppose."

"And our continued pursuit of these ideals indicates that we believe the answers to our problems exist, right?"

"Yeah..."

"But how close is science to obtaining that perfection? Judging from how close we are to curing all disease or ending all conflict world-wide, how close are we to this goal?"

"Well, not very close at all, I guess," admitted Logic.

"So why do we put so much faith in it?" asked Life.

"I don't know," conceded Logic. "I guess because sometimes it's all we have to cling to; all we have to put faith in."

"Is it?" asked Life. "I see another option—a higher power who happens to know all the answers to the science of our universe. He knows everything we have discovered and everything we haven't yet. Admittedly the knowledge exists; we just can't admit that we humans don't have the answers. Man's goal is to accumulate everything; knowledge, power, and prestige. Ultimately, we want to become like God, but we can't admit that he exists."

"Compelling," responded Logic, obviously evaluating.

"Let me ask you something, Logic," said Life. "If you had the ability to create life, would you? If you had the ability to mastermind an entire existence, would you do it?"

"Of course," said Logic. "Who wouldn't?"

"And don't you believe that the most rewarding things that your theoretical creation could do, if it could possibly have the capacity, is to recognize the beauty of your plan? That is all our Creator requires of us; that we recognize his creation, his plan, as superior to ours. Once we make that realization, things start to fall into place."

Logic sat perplexed for a moment, and finally came to a conclusion. "Alright, I'm on board with the church idea, just because I want to see how this 'search for hope' shakes out, but it's purely experimental, in the interest of science. And we still have some talking to do."

"Agreed," said Life optimistically.

"Are you two done?" asked Pleasure miserably. "We're starting to have these meetings every three months? You guys are really getting on my nerves here. And now we're going to church, hey? Not if I can help it."

"Even *you* know something is wrong here, Pleasure," said Life. "And we are trying church as a means to correct it. Nothing is working. The Committee has higher hopes than it has had in a while, but our situation is still dismal. We need to do something to correct it, or the consequences could be devastating."

"I *am* doing something to correct it," said Pleasure. "I'm getting high. Meeting adjourned." He stood up and stormed out of the boardroom.

chapter 11: **holy ping-pong**

After debating for a month or two, I finally decided to go try out this church early in the spring of 2004. My life was a mess, and I was feeling like crap. What did I have to lose, besides an hour and a little sleep? The website said that the church had an 11:30 a.m. service, perfect for a drunk like me.

The first Sunday I intended to go, I didn't. I decided that my sleep was just a little more important to me, and that perhaps 11:30 a.m. was too early for a drunk like me. Several Sundays I put off going, usually because I was hung over from Saturday night. But one Sunday, I finally got my lazy butt up and drove the twenty minutes across town to the church.

It looked even bigger than it had on the website. The size was intimidating to me at first; was this huge church going to collectively condemn me? Was I walking into a building full of people who would think I was the scum of the earth? Still, I had driven this far; I parked and proceeded into the church.

The mood was warm and inviting as I entered the church, welcomed by the people stationed at the door. A hearty handshake, and a quick "how are you today?" were all part of the semi-professional world that I was well-equipped to deal with. *At least they didn't hug me,* I thought. I walked into the enormous sanctuary, and sunk into a pew close to the back, ready to observe the ceremony. Besides the greeters, no one seemed to notice me, which I didn't mind. I really liked the option to hide among the masses; nobody could point me out as a poser. I readied myself to perform a complete analysis of the experience. The service got under way.

The music was fast-paced and uplifting. It sounded something like my dad's backwoods Pentecostal church, but the musicians put on a higher-caliber performance. It was almost like a concert with encouraged audience participation. I didn't recognize any of the songs, but they had a modern, contemporary beat, and the words were posted on several huge projector screens so I could sing along if I wanted to. I didn't want to. I enjoyed the music, but it definitely wasn't something I'd listen to in my spare time.

Next came the offering, and I thought to myself, *This is where they get you.* And I was right; they gave a little mini-sermon on how "you will be blessed if you give." I thought it was a little ulterior-motived, but I supposed that even the church was a business that needed money to survive. Nobody would condemn a charity for asking for donations, and a church supposedly would have similar positive intentions. And it was a huge facility, after all. I wasn't worried about contributing, seeing as I was staying true to my token gifts to my dad's church each month. But I sure wasn't feeling those "blessings" they were preaching about.

During the offering, the projectors for the song words were used to post various church events. I watched the brief, one-frame advertisements, and was surprised at how many mid-week events this church had. There were classes, Bible studies, game nights, prayer meetings, and countless other activities. I wasn't interested after the first several, so I only paid half-attention as the listings continued. Then one event caught my eye.

"Ping-Pong, 7:00 p.m. Tuesday nights, Room 4." That sounded like fun. I hadn't played ping-pong in any regularity for years. My dad had taught me the game when I was a kid, and we spent a lot of quality time together in my grandma's basement, at either end of a beat-up ping-pong table. His patience with my development eventually turned me into a decent player. I thought it might be fun to try my hand against some of the church "locals."

Soon the offering was over, and the sermon commenced. There behind the pulpit, and sometimes wandering around the platform, was the author of the book I had read. He looked a little older than his picture, and seemed to be a good-humored fellow. He gave his sermon, and it was entertaining and educational. I didn't retain much, but I didn't get too bored either. I left church, and gave the experience about a "B+." I quickly returned home to the normalcy of my depression.

That week, I gave "ping-pong night" a try. The church had been warm and receptive enough, so maybe the ping-pong guys would be too. I walked into the room, and met the "gang." Most of the guys were older than me by at least twenty years, but that sure didn't mean they couldn't compete. Some guys I could beat, and some guys beat me handily. We played for almost two hours; singles, then doubles, then a new "cut-throat" game I had never played before. I had a great time, and the guys seemed to like my competition as well. I excitedly assured them I would be back.

A few days later, I got a letter from the County, indicating that I was charged with possession of marijuana, and that I was supposed to call and schedule a meeting with the lady who would set up my case. I called her and shortly after that I visited her office in the courthouse building downtown. My first impression of this woman was that she had dealt with many failures like me before. She did not come across as very optimistic about my life. Especially when I truthfully answered the question "When was the last time you smoked marijuana?" It had been a few days.

She laid my options out for me. My first option was to go to court, and accept whatever the judge decided to give me as a penalty, at his discretion, with no appeal available. This meant that the offense may or may not stay on my record, depending on what he deemed appropriate. The second option was the "Diversion Program," in which I would have a hefty fine, forty hours of community service, random drug testing starting weekly, six months probation, and some drug "homework" I would have to complete. With this option, if I finished the six months successfully, the offense would be wiped from my record. I could choose now, or defer my decision for thirty days so I could "think about it."

I thought about it. The judge was an unsure outcome, but if he was looking at me anything like this lady was, he would probably see what a loser I was and give me a hefty penalty for my deviance. On the other hand, the probation option was a pretty weighty penalty as well, but there was no uncertainty in the outcome, except whether or not I could make it through the program. And the pot I had just smoked a few days earlier was still in my system, as far as drug testing was concerned. In order to pass the first test, I would have to defer the decision for as long as I could, and then choose the probation. So that is exactly what I did.

The penalty for failing to complete the "Diversion Program" was that I would be forced to sit before the judge, and it would also be entered as evidence that I had failed the probation program. In other words, he would likely punish me to the fullest extent, including permanently attaching the offense to my record. Once he did that, my chances of getting any professional job would be slim, if I'd have to check the "yes" box for convictions. So once enrolled in the program, smoking pot would be the utter destruction of my hope for a reputable career. As if it hadn't been destructive enough to me without that addition.

The drug homework taught me nothing. I labored through it contemptuously, and had it done in no time. The fine cramped me a little, but with the help of a few extra shifts at the party store I wrapped it up without much trouble... and again learned nothing. The drug testing was humiliating; I had to have an employee of the clinic standing there watching me pee into a cup each week. If I didn't participate wholeheartedly with that I would be in big trouble. Given the threat of the judge, I finally had a binding reason to stop smoking weed. I stayed clean, because I had to. I figured that the community service was going to be about the same as the fine: put in my hours, do my duty, and get out the door. I signed up for a local soup kitchen.

Once at the soup kitchen, I saw a group of people similar to the party store "regular" crowd. Again, it was the socially dejected group, but this time the role I played in their lives was different. I wasn't selling them more disparity, like the kind found in a life of liquor. Instead, I was giving them nourishment—what they needed to live. I worked alongside other offenders, many with chips on their shoulders. Opposite to them were the volunteer workers contributing their time simply out of kindness. They were happy to be there, and I started to figure out why. Helping those less-fortunate people made me feel good. I was forced to do it, and I would never have chosen it as my Saturday morning activity. And yet, I enjoyed parts of it, more than I enjoyed most other aspects of my life at the time. Why did giving feel so good?

During the early months of my probation, I attempted to visit the church on occasion, but was too lazy most of the time. But I wouldn't miss ping-pong. I got to know the guys pretty well as we went back-and-forth in our epic battles, sharpening up our skills together. Many "pongers" came and went, but we had a core group, and I was one of them. It felt good to belong to something positive. On Tuesdays, resisting drinking and smoking was just a little bit easier.

Between ping-pong and the soup kitchen, I started to feel just a touch of joy returning to my life. I had subjected myself to some positive influence, and some I was forced into, but regardless, the effects were starting to manifest in my happiness. My weed use had been cut down to zero, and alcohol just wasn't as fun without weed. Because my "less-positive" party circle of friends always had weed, I had to stay sober enough that I could still resist getting high, which meant I couldn't get as hammered as I had liked to before. And drinking by itself, without pot as an "equalizer," left me feeling dismal. Pot and alcohol had become a team, and without both of them, they began to lose their grip on me. I started to feel free.

At my day job, I was still on a different kind of probation due to my shoddy performance. One of my coworkers knew I was having problems getting along with my boss and she sent me an e-mail that had a job-posting website on it. I went to the site, and saw a pretty decent job that would utilize my background a little more effectively than my current job. The only problem was that the company was known for being difficult to get hired into. I had heard stories about several of my coworkers applying many times and being rejected. *What the heck?* I thought. I threw together a résumé and had to send it overnight mail just to have the hope of getting it in under their deadline. I didn't know if it made it in on time, or if they would even consider me, or if my possession charge would ruin my chances.

Late that spring, after about two-and-a-half months of passed drug tests, the testing became less frequent and was cut back to about once a month, still randomly. But knowing the tests were monthly opened up a small window of opportunity for me, and I again started to consider smoking pot occasionally with my friends. Apparently, I didn't learn my lesson yet. The common belief was that pot stayed in the human system for about a month after use, so once I got tested, in theory, I could smoke a few times before I had to quit for another month in preparation to pass my next test. This little system seemed to be quite promising to me. So one Friday, I went in for my drug test, passed, and then proceeded to my friend's house to smoke some pot and get drunk. We partied it up for the entire weekend, and I was thinking I had at least a month before I would be tested, and probably had time for a few more smoke-sessions.

That week, I was surprised to get a call from the company for which I had applied a few weeks before. They wanted an interview. I tried not to act too excited, and I set up the interview for the next week. I went out and bought a nice new shirt and tie, and did a little half-effort interview preparation.

Once there, the interview was a disaster from my viewpoint. They wanted specific examples of how I had well-applied my job skills in the past, and I couldn't come up with much. My past job-related irresponsibility left me with little to work with. I became frustrated, but hung in there until they were done. I shook their hands with a big fake smile and returned to my car. *Crap!* I thought.

To my amazement, they called shortly after to offer me the job with my begin-date only two weeks away. The manager said he'd give me time to think about it, and would provide me with more details when I called back.

I was dumbfounded, but overjoyed to hear such wonderful news. I quickly and happily submitted my two-week notice to the boss with whom I was having the problems. I called back the manager from the new job, and accepted the position. He told me that the only stipulation was a mandatory drug test to be conducted next week. My heart sank, knowing I had smoked weed the past weekend, and that the test would be at max two weeks from my last smoke date. On top of that, he also mentioned that they had to conduct a background search before I could start. He said he was confident neither would be a problem. With him on the phone, and the job offer in place, I couldn't do anything but agree.

My heart sank even further when I found out that my random turn had also come up for my probation drug-testing in the same week. I was going to be in big trouble. My life was about to change; in two weeks I would be jobless, and who knew what the judge was going to sentence me to once I failed that drug test? So I had nothing I could do, nowhere I could turn, except maybe this God I had visited at church. So I started to pray.

The first thing I did was admit that I was a failure and a moron for still smoking after it was so blatantly destroying everything in my life. I cried to God, asking him to set things right, asking him to forgive my weakness, and promising to do better if only he would let me pass the drug tests. I asked him to help me with my drug and alcohol problems, by whatever means necessary. I prayed many times throughout the week, and then I headed to my drug testing, terrified.

Tension was at an all-time high when I peed into the cup, two tests in the same day. I knew the prayer hadn't worked, and I knew I was going to have to start working full-time at the liquor store, best-case scenario. Those drug tests were just a formality to my downfall. *At least I had my alcohol and pot to fall back on,* I thought to myself. They'd always be there.

Somehow, I beat the odds, and both my drug tests came back negative. To my further amazement, the company called me back and said all things were in order, no mention of my offense, and I signed some papers and became an official member of their team. My new job put me back to the "professional" level, and had better pay, benefits, and vacation time than any job I had ever had before. Plus the people I worked with were great, and my new boss and I became good friends, especially when I flexed some of my computer skills. I had to ask myself, *did God answer my prayer?* My happiness was returning and a new hope was growing inside me. I had gone from the brink of destruction, from thoughts of suicide, to a new low level of success and revitalized happiness. And though it made no logical sense, the catalyst seemed to somehow be going to church and helping others. I decided I would have to spend more time doing both, to see if this positive trend continued.

Society had first been completely cynical about going
to church, but had to admit the crowd was a little more
trendy and "normal" than his original stereotypes. The
music had been generally appealing—again a surprise to
Society. When the offering started, Society had jumped
on his opportunity to point out the fact that they truly
did want my money. But the sermon had been amusing
and understandable, and for the most part Society hadn't
made that big of a fuss.

On the other hand, there had been nothing for
Pleasure at the church. He hadn't enjoyed a minute of it,
constantly complaining about how he was missing out
on sleep. He had criticized the people, the music, and the
sermon, but Society hadn't been paying as much attention to him.

For years, Society had thought he had people in general figured out, but here was a new group that he'd never
really analyzed or incorporated into his opinion. He had
received a lot of input from my friends. They usually
thought God was silliness, for the foolish who couldn't
accept the thought of their own death. Somehow, these
friends were smarter than the "believers," and yet, he
watched many of these friends betray me or end up in
trouble or jail or worse. In fact, I had betrayed people,
and I was in trouble, and I was convinced that worse was
on the way if I didn't do something. Society truly cared
about my friends, and he loved their company, but he

could not vindicate the path they were taking. He couldn't fully identify with them anymore, now that Conscience had finally spoken up

It intrigued Society to see this church group with morals almost opposite of the ones he had come to understand, but a group that still seemed to fit into society. He had known some religious "crazies" from my dad's church, who couldn't even fit in with the social mainstream. And the people at my mom's church were the opposite—very professional and socially accepted, but seemingly unexcited about God. The people at this new church, however, seemed to have both high enthusiasm levels and the ability to meld with the real world. Society thought maybe he could fit in there, social acceptance being his highest goal.

The six-month review was called to order, and Life started immediately discussing the church. "Wow, I really like that church group, and that ping-pong group too. What do you think, Society?"

"I don't understand what's so intriguing about them," puzzled Society, still analyzing.

Life began to elaborate on the uniqueness of the church. "Most social groups are brought together by location or convenience, like neighbors or coworkers, or common-activity-interest groups. That's where most of our friends have come from—a shared enjoyment of partying. But the church was not built on anything so temporary or coincidental. The church was built on morals—on common beliefs for human behavior. Everybody slips up from time to time, but the church is a structured system to support *not* slipping up—to support doing the right thing. Messing up and admitting it is much more powerful than hiding our faults, though it is initially more painful. But according to their rules, the church *has* to accept others, regardless of short-comings. That is what makes this group so unique and powerful; they don't subscribe to the tactics of normal society."

"But sometimes normal society helps us to figure out an acceptable path to take," countered Pleasure.

"True enough, but if normal society knew exactly how we've spent so many nights, with continued drug abuse and drunk driving, what would they do with us?" asked Life.

"Who cares? The ones that do know, think it's cool," responded Pleasure.

"But if police or employers really caught on to our abuse of our privileges, don't you think we'd be sent to jail, or rehab, or fired, at least?" asked Life.

"Maybe, but they're not going to find out," replied Pleasure arrogantly.

"But that's the difference between the church and the 'real world'," said Life. "By the law, we are guilty of a lot more than we've been caught for. And by social standards, by the book, being guilty requires our punishment. But the beauty of the church is that by their book, we can be guilt-free as long as we change our ways. Even if the people of the church wanted to hold something against us, ultimately they will have to admit that doing so is wrong."

"Unconditional acceptance..." mused Society.

"That's right," said Life. "Available to anyone."

Pleasure saw that the tide was turning for Society and spoke up. "Logic, can you tell Life how it really is? He seems to be neck-deep in pixie dust."

"Okay, Life, if the church is built on the same moral base, then why are there so many denominations out there? Which one is right?" questioned Logic, on cue.

"The same reason that there are so many people out there, and not one is always 'right.' Each person has a hundred different relationships, and each one is unique. Step one is to seek God, and step two is to find a church that expresses yourself and your style to him. Just because we don't like Mom or Dad's churches doesn't mean God isn't there; it just means that our preferable place of joy would involve social consciousness *and* high enthusiasm. Some people like to shake God's hand, and others like to give him a high-five. Neither is wrong, and there are still common threads among all Christian moral sets, despite the differences in doctrine. We know that the Greater Good is bigger than all of us, so we need to be around people that maximize our understanding of its potential. A group based on 'good' is a great start."

"You still haven't convinced me that God exists," said Logic. "He still doesn't make sense to me."

"It is imperative that you flex a little faith—that is what God is looking for," said Life. "For example, look at the results of the illogical but faith-based move of Finance. Small contributions over the years, and suddenly we have moved into a new higher-paying job."

"That isn't connected," retorted Logic. "At best, it was coincidence; our break was just due."

"And I suppose the crash that facilitated the move was a coincidence, and the New Year's bust that forced reduced pot smoking was a coincidence," returned Life.

"Yeah, pretty much."

"So how many more coincidences will it take until you believe that God is working behind the scenes?" asked Life. "At what point does it become illogical to believe these are just coincidences?"

"How about one more good coincidence?" said Logic sarcastically. "I've told you before; there is too much scientific evidence against God, and not enough for him. I still think there's a high probability that God was 'created' as a means for humankind to deal with the fact that our lives will end, and we just can't accept it."

"Sure, that's often the original motivation for choosing God's way—the hope of heaven," answered Life. "Undoubtedly, the results of our life will have either positive, negative, or zero effect on the future. But the good or bad things we do have potential to live beyond our death, much like the men and women who have shaped our history. Is it so hard to believe that the same good or bad we create can extend even beyond *human* existence? Yes, preachers use the hope of heaven or the threat of hell to motivate people to live for God, but regardless of what we think about the afterlife, all we truly have any control over is life right now. I'm not asking you to believe in heaven or hell or any of that; I'm asking you to start looking for God. Start searching for him for the sake of this life, not necessarily the future one. Yes, heaven is real and so is hell, but right now we need God more than we need to worry about the afterlife. Please just support the positive influence church gives off, and we can debate after we gather more input."

"Your logic is poor," said Logic, "but I can't argue with the fact that continued change is necessary, and that Pleasure is running us into the ground with his exploits. I will accept deference of this controversy until more non-scientific evidence is gathered, and I will accept church as a source of this evidence."

"Yeah, church is okay by me too," said Society humbly. "I think there's a lot I can learn from this group of people, even if none of it is logic-based. These people carry themselves differently, and I want to find out why. I want to find out if they're real."

Pleasure didn't say a word as he watched his dynasty crumbling. Church was no fun and neither was discipline, or kindness, and the whole situation reeked of those. But Pleasure hadn't given up hope yet. His grip was strong, and he still had overruling power on the Committee. He sat there waiting for an opportune moment to launch a counterstrike against these rebels, and silence them all. And the perfect opportunity was only a few months down the road.

"Are you through?" he asked, unamused. "Now we're going to start attending church regularly, I assume? Great work guys," he said cynically. "Meeting adjourned."

chapter 12: **warning track**

Over the course of the summer of 2004, my happiness was slowly re-accumulating. My new job was going great, and I was making a lot of new work friends. I was attending church more regularly and was building positive friendships there as well. I had shifted my monthly contributions to my new church, and I was really making an effort to get involved. I was even reading the Bible and praying regularly—sometimes. And my major downfall of the last five years, smoking pot and drinking, was at an all-time low. My alcohol consumption was on the weekends at most, and oftentimes I went for weeks without. Pot smoking was even less; though the drug testing was tapering off, I still had to report from time to time. I never had any personal pot since I couldn't smoke regularly. I was only smoking occasionally, bumming both pot and cigarettes from friends.

Late that summer, I moved out of the apartment my girlfriend had left me with and into a much cheaper apartment complex across town. My new one-bedroom lodging was a small third-story apartment in a less classy neighborhood, but I didn't care. It was cheap, and closer to work. My church attendance continued to grow, as my party attendance lessened.

I really enjoyed my party friends but I found myself, often out of necessity, avoiding them. I was never sure how well I would be able to hold up from weekend to weekend against the peer pressure to participate. They knew I was on probation, and so they tried to make it easier on me by not offering me any pot, but every time a joint was going around, I wanted to grab it and take a puff. Given my weakness to this temptation, I was often forced to abstain from the group. I missed them, but I had to do what I felt was right. And I knew that staying away from pot, and alcohol, was best for me in the long run. I was struggling, but this time I was winning.

By the fall of 2004, I was attending church every Sunday, sometimes after a Saturday night of falling to my temptations. Regardless, my failures were diminishing, and really I felt like I was making progress, given the discipline it took to make myself get up Sunday mornings. I was also trying very hard to do a good job at work, which called for good discipline as well. I hadn't called in sick once since I had my new job, and it was a rarity that I even had one beer on a weeknight.

In early November, the day I had been anxiously awaiting finally arrived. My six months were up, and I was off probation. No more fines, or drug tests, or community service. The aftermath of the New Year's adventure was finally over. I signed the papers, bid farewell to the probation lady, and ventured freely out into the world.

I found myself standing before a fork in life's road. My new more-sober lifestyle was going pretty well; I had built a solid base in both professionalism and at the church. I actually had some friends who didn't want me to get drunk, though few knew I even had a problem. Part of me didn't want to let my new friends down, but then again, I felt like I was abandoning my party friends if I didn't tear it up with them sometimes. I didn't know which way to go, but I had a whole lot less reason to avoid those parties now that probation was over.

The weekend after I got off probation I headed back to the party group to celebrate my freedom. I tried to mention the church and how well my life was going since I had been seeking God, but I knew they thought I was acting weird. I also tried to be resistant to the pot and alcohol, with limited success. I eventually made a deal with my best friend that I would party with him if he would go to church with me on Sunday. And both of us followed through. My friend agreed that the church was mildly entertaining, but it was just "not for him." I respected his opinion. But I began to realize that if I didn't want to drink and smoke, I couldn't hang around him or the party group anymore, period. It certainly wasn't because I didn't want to, but I was just too weak to say "no."

One Sunday, late in November, I came home from church and found myself in the solitude of my apartment, really craving some pot. I convinced myself that after all that probation I had earned a bag. I was sick of all the sober Sunday evenings, and though I tried to resist it, I called a buddy of mine to see if he had any pot for sale. He did, and he also mentioned that he had the "good stuff," which was essentially higher-caliber weed at fifty bucks an eighth. I told him I would be over in a few minutes.

I don't know how many times my mind told me not to do it as I walked out the door and down the stairs to my car. I had to fight through it just to open my car door. *A little music will clear this up,* I thought as I put the key into the ignition. I turned it, but my Grand Am wouldn't turn over. I tried again and again, with no success.

Up until that point, I hadn't had any trouble with the car whatsoever. I had just driven it back from church less than an hour ago. But now, for some reason, it wouldn't start. Feeling an anger comparable to "the Christmas of realization," I opened the hood and frogged around with the engine for a few minutes, though I knew nothing of cars. I got the manual out, and tried to solve the problem, with no luck. The whole time I was thinking, *I really shouldn't be buying any drugs.* Frustrated, I went back to my apartment to cool off and think about what was going on.

date: november 21, 2004
purpose: emergency meeting
agenda: chairman pleasure's new program

The mood of the Committee had been at an all-time high during the fall of 2004. Happiness was again becoming an active member of the deliberations, and the meetings were becoming less hostile as discontentment dispersed. Most everyone liked the way things were going, with the only exception being Pleasure. He didn't like the new brand of decision-making that often left him out of the loop. So he had been watching silently, waiting for an opportunity to regain power.

Since the conversion of Society, Logic was the only remaining member besides Pleasure who was not in agreement with the "God program." He was definitely forced to admit that things were going better and better as more members agreed to follow God, but he was still certain that these good things were coincidental. Life had put up some good arguments for his cause, but Logic just couldn't let go of his clinging doubt. That November's meeting, however, was Pleasure-driven.

"Okay, you morons," Pleasure said to the Committee. "I've sat here watching you disrespect me for way too long, and now is the rebirth of the season of Pleasure. Now you will all recognize my power. We're going back to the way it was before any of this started, before you opened your big mouth, Conscience. It's time to return to the party life!"

"You overestimate your power," said Life. He quickly turned to Logic, who was always ripe for debate. "Logic, do you still think that all of this is chance? This life, this earth, and this universe?"

"Yes, I do," replied Logic, "and I really have seen no evidence to the contrary."

"And 'chaos' makes sense to you as a human origin?" asked Life.

"More sense than 'magic'," answered Logic.

"Do you remember our first car?" asked Life, apparently changing the subject.

"Uh, yeah," replied Logic, a little thrown-off.

"What a beautiful sight that faded-red Reliant was to seventeen-year-old eyes," reminisced Life. "Where is that car today?"

"What on earth.... ?" asked Logic.

"Humor me," said Life. "Where is that car right now?"

"At Dad's house, I guess," answered Logic, still hesitant. "Sitting in the field, rusting. Why do you ask?"

"It certainly is rusting; decaying away," Life agreed. "In fact, the same is true of everything on this earth; it will all eventually decay. Eventually, there will be nothing left in that field, as the car disintegrates completely. Its natural tendency is to fall apart."

"So what?" said Logic.

"So why do you believe that out of chaos, in a universe with constant laws and a tendency toward disorder, the complete opposite could happen?" asked Life.

"What do you mean?" asked Logic.

"How could this universe just appear out of thin air, in contradiction to everything we know about nature's laws?" inquired Life. "This earth is a beautiful symmetry of life, and you're telling me that chaos just by chance put it together? That's like telling me that the car in the field could 'build itself' under the right circumstances of chance. But every human knows the only way that car gets built is with the addition of intelligent life into the equation. And the only thing that could keep that car from rusting is continued maintenance, again from intelligent life. How could you believe otherwise?"

"Okay, okay, the 'Big Bang' is a little far-fetched, but you can't discount the scientific evidence that Evolution presents," retorted Logic.

"Oh, Evolution is a little more believable," said Life.

"Really?" said Logic, surprised. "So you believe God set up the universe, and then the animals took it from there?"

"Oh no, God is still in complete control," answered Life. "I just see why the idea of Evolution is so appealing, because it is true in some part. You see, God has a thinking process much like ours. So when he decided he was going to create the earth, he did some thinking and planning. His first thoughts and plans began with the container for life—the cell. He developed the idea more and more, from single-celled animals to more complex ones. Eventually, as his ideas evolved, he thought up mammals, and primates, and finally humans. And then he created it all."

"That's a little far-fetched," responded Logic.

"I just want you to be thinking, Logic," said Life. "You act like God and science conflict at every turn, but there is truthfully an amazing union of the two that is our reality. Just think, if God did exist, how would the world be different? How would you visualize the earth if he was in complete control?"

"There sure wouldn't be all this depression and death," answered Logic. "There would be peace and happiness as far as the eye could see."

"Sounds like you're describing the typical depiction of heaven," said Life, "with unity and happiness galore. But don't you think that developing a civilization like that would require some preparation? Certainly not one human comes into this world ready to live in a utopia like that. We're too imperfect. My observation is that this lifetime is the practice round for that 'perfect society.' We have one life to practice and display that we are ready for that world. The alternative is of course 'not ready,' in which case the unprepared must be discarded for the sake of achieving perfection in that future society. Everything on this earth makes perfect sense, if you have the right understanding. Happiness cannot be fully appreciated until it is chosen and developed."

"That's quite a rant," said Logic, again contemplating.

"Just think about it," said Life. "I can assure you that God is the right choice, but belief is something that needs to be developed too. Even if you agree with me today, you still may doubt at some point in the future. But I'm working on that..."

"What do you mean?" questioned Logic.

"Will you two shut up?" asked Pleasure angrily. "Your little rebellion is about to end anyway, Life, so don't get too comfortable."

"Pleasure, I know you try to do the right thing, but you're just too simple-minded," replied Life. "You can't see the big picture."

"*You're* about to see the big picture, Life!" scoffed Pleasure. "We're going back to the party life, no matter what you say!"

"Don't do it, Pleasure," said Life. "This isn't what we want and this isn't even what you want. You are being controlled. You have to understand this."

"*I* control my own destiny!" shouted Pleasure. "No one else!"

"Then who is that behind you?" asked Life.

"What are you talking about?" asked Pleasure, puzzled.

"Yeah, I see them too," said Logic, completely perplexed. Nervous whispers ran through the Committee as the other members slowly noticed the uninvited guests. "Who are they, Pleasure?" asked Logic.

"I don't know!" exclaimed Pleasure, frustrated.

"You know, if you really think about it," said Life.

"No, I don't!" denied Pleasure vehemently.

"Show yourselves!" shouted Life.

From the dark corner behind Pleasure emerged three sinister figures. The first two were skinny men, both pale and wrinkled, and probably around sixty years old. Their age didn't show in their walk or their mannerisms as they stepped smoothly up to the table on either side of Pleasure. The men had short gray hair, and wore sharp black suits and sunglasses. The third figure was a very attractive woman with long wavy blonde hair and a curvy figure, tightly confined in a black business suit with a very short skirt. She stood directly behind Pleasure, with her hands on his shoulders. The taller man responded with a deeply relaxed tone: "You called?"

Pleasure looked to his sides and behind him. "What the... Who are you?" Pleasure demanded angrily.

"Life is right, my little puppet," the dark man continued, in monotone. "You don't even have control over yourself anymore. We have been using your weak discretion to run this Committee from the sidelines for a while now. We applaud you; we really haven't had to do much work at all. But I suppose if Life is going to call us out, we might as well take it from here."

"What... what do you mean?" stammered Pleasure.

"Poor little dense Pleasure," said the shorter man. "So full of vitality, but so simple-minded. It should be obvious to anyone who we are and what our purpose is."

"Who are you?" asked Pleasure.

"They are the habits that you let take over, Pleasure," interjected Life sorrowfully. "Alcohol, Pot, and Lust."

"You did a great job, Honey," Lust whispered in Pleasure's ear.

"Ah, Life, so perceptive," mocked Alcohol, the taller of the two men. "You had an idea what was going on ever since Conscience opened his big mouth, didn't you? It's too bad for your little Committee that Pleasure was so strong, or you might have had a chance."

"We still have a chance," said Life weakly.

"Oh, oh, I'm sorry, that's the wrong answer," said Pot condescendingly. "You *had* a chance, but all of that is over now. You led a nice campaign, Life, but you lose. You gave Pleasure and Logic quite a run for their money, what with all the moving and shaking you've done. A lot of decent coincidences backed you up, but through them all, Pleasure and Logic 'fought the rebellion.' Don't worry," he said turning to Pleasure and Logic, "under our regime, we'll take care of you both. But these others will not be so fortunate."

"No, no, this isn't right," said Pleasure, frightened. "I change my vote. I'm on Life's side now."

"Sorry fellas, the ballots have already been counted," said Alcohol. "And we're in by a nose."

"I'm so sorry, Life," said Pleasure dejectedly. "I never... I never meant..."

"It's okay," consoled Life quietly.

"So, what are you going to do with us?" asked Logic, starting to get nervous.

"Good old Logic," replied Alcohol. "Stuck in his weak mindset to the very end. Are you stupid or something?" shouted Alcohol angrily, his face contorting. "The signs are all here! We've been actively doing what we are going to do for the last four-plus years! You pride yourself on being 'so smart,' but your eyes are shut, pal. Everything in your life has been getting worse since we've been in the picture. We wrecked Health, hurt Finance, and abolished Happiness! It should be obvious by now; we are here to destroy you! And now it's way too late to change that. You had your chance. But now, we're taking over. And our first order is to get rid of Life! Come on," he gestured to Pot.

The two shady men approached Life, and grabbed his arms aggressively. The other members watched in horror, too scared to move. Life didn't put up much of a fight, but he shouted to the Committee as he was being dragged toward the door, "Please, you guys, don't give up hope. Hang in there, you'll be alright."

"I won't give up hope, Life," cried Happiness from the table.

"Yes, you will," scoffed Alcohol, elbowing Life in the mouth. The two men proceeded to drag Life to the door, but they weren't done with him yet.

"Look, Committee, here's your 'mighty hero'," hissed Pot as they threw Life face-first into the wall beside the door. Life collapsed to the floor, spots of his blood staining the wall. "You're going to 'find the way,' are you, Life?" Pot went on. "You're going to 'fix things up'? Fix yourself, Mr. Revolutionary. You can't even get up."

Life slowly lifted himself up from the ground and stood to his feet. With blood trickling out of his nose and mouth, he stared Alcohol right in the face with a look of determination. Happiness couldn't take it any more. He stood up and ran toward the three men. Life noticed him quickly and broke the stare-down with Alcohol.

"No, Happiness," said Life, "not right now. Please, my friend, you have to trust me." The two dark men turned around and glared at the boy. He didn't look at them at all. His lower lip trembled slightly, but he maintained his gaze at Life.

"I'll do whatever you say," Happiness replied quietly. He returned to his seat at the table, tears in his eyes. And Alcohol and Pot returned to their cruelty. The other members sat frozen in fear, with no idea how to combat such a hostile takeover. Pot grabbed Life's arms and held them back. With an evil gleam of enjoyment in his eyes, Alcohol began punching Life in the stomach and face over and over.

"You're worthless, you're hopeless, you're archaic, and you're unneeded," Alcohol chided as he continued the beating, with Pot urging him on.

Life was not holding up so well under the intense attacks. His clothes were torn and his face was covered in blood. Finally Alcohol got bored with the punching. He turned back to the Committee, his fists stained from the pummeling. Pot dropped Life to the ground. Life laid there in agony, coughing and wheezing.

"This could be any one of you," said Alcohol, addressing the table. "In answer to your question, Logic, *this* is what we came to do." He turned around and kicked Life violently in the face, snapping his neck back, and leaving him bloody and motionless on the floor. The dark men grabbed his arms and threw his limp body roughly out the door of the boardroom, slamming it tight.

"Don't worry, Baby," Lust said, consoling a mortified Pleasure. "We're going to take care of you now. You get everything you wanted; we *are* going to return to the party life."

Pot returned to his spot beside Pleasure, and Alcohol sat down in Life's chair. "A few things around here are going to change now," he said. "Now you can see our power, our strength. We can do more than just shout, we can rough you up or kick you out, if necessary. So my advice is that you listen to us, or your fate will be the same as Life's."

"You're a bad man," said little Happiness.

"Oh, you poor little guy," said Alcohol. "You really liked Life, didn't you?" He slapped Happiness across the face. "I don't show mercy to the ignorant!" he growled. "You all must obey me!" Happiness started crying.

"Go easy on them, Honey," said Lust to Alcohol. She gave Happiness a little kiss-gesture with her big red lips. He kept crying.

"Okay, the first order of business is to go get those drugs, and some beer, and do this Sunday up right!" said Alcohol. "I'll give you all about a week to ease into our leadership, but after that, any insubordination will be crushed. We will meet again to discuss the future in less than two weeks. Meeting adjourned!"

The members sat around the table in shock, scarcely able to comprehend what had just happened. "Well, get out of here!" shouted Pot. The members scurried from their seats and out the door.

"That went well," said Alcohol to his cohorts with an evil smile.

chapter 13: **the push**

About twenty minutes after my car problems, I went back downstairs to the parking lot to try it again. The car started right away. I drove to my friend's place and paid my fifty bucks. We smoked a little, though I really just wanted to get home and smoke by myself. After paying my social dues, I left for my apartment.

On the way back home I stopped by a store and picked up a six-pack, and some pornography, which had filled the role of "girlfriend" in my life from time to time during my depression. I got home, still pretty high, and smoked some more. After a lengthy period of limiting my pot and alcohol to social events, I got drunk sitting alone in my new apartment, like I had so many times before at my old apartment. The hole I thought I had crawled out of enveloped me again. Anything positive that church had given me that morning was obliterated. I immediately started feeling depressed again. That night, I went to bed in a haze that was all too familiar. I continued to live in this familiar haze for the next week.

After months of what seemed like progress, I once again re-entered the destructive lifestyle that had unraveled me before. The discipline I built up had only limited strength against my desire to drink and smoke. I was right at the edge, ready to jump into a new positive phase of my life, but my past habits didn't want me to go. So I again catered to their desires. I again fell back into a familiarly hopeless pit, which this time seemed more dismal than before.

The idea that God was there, deeper than I could ever truly grasp, had somehow become acceptable. I had spent some time with his people at the church, and had a sense of who they thought God was, and the good things he had in store for me. But I needed one more part. I needed to know for sure God was watching out for me, that he wasn't just some creation of my mind to cope with pain or death. The evidence of God in my life was really starting to accumulate, but I still had reservations.

I knew the road I had been down so many times before, with the alcohol and drugs, and it provided me with an element of security. I knew exactly what was going to happen to me physically when I drank or inhaled. I knew I was failing, but the certainty made it easier to accept this failure. Accepting failure took an immediate toll. I didn't want to see any of my new friends. I didn't want to go to ping-pong or church or work. I didn't want to face humanity. I just wanted to stew in my failure—to curl up with my addiction and die. Complacency again started to rule me.

For the first time since I was hired to my new job, I called in sick. I sat home that day at the end of November, smoking pot and drinking, playing video games and watching the clock slowly tick away. I was worried that someone was going to stop by to see me deep in my secret despair. At the same time, I needed help from somewhere. I called out to God, asking for his help to rid me of this problem. When I received no answer by bedtime, I smoked another joint, and set the roach on my lamp stand. I sauntered into my bedroom and crashed for the night.

Shortly after midnight, I sat up in bed. Something woke me up, but I didn't know what. I looked around in the dark, still a little high and unsure of what was going on. Suddenly, the quiet of the night was shattered by rapping at my door. I wondered who it could be at this time of night, and got a little nervous, buying into my mom's fear of the neighborhood. I slowly made my way to the door, still half-asleep and looked out the peephole. It was completely dark. I unlocked the door and opened it a crack.

And a crack was all they needed. The door flung open and a gang of masked men were on top of me blinding me with flashlights. They held me down with clear plastic shields, shouting "Police, search warrant!" over and over. I was pinned down and cuffed as they searched for the light switch and checked my apartment for other "perpetrators."

"Is anyone else in here?" one of them shouted gruffly.

"No," I responded truthfully.

They stood me up and made me stand face-against-the-wall, still cuffed, and in my underwear, while one of them read me my rights. He didn't let me look around much, but I could see about ten cops roaming through my small apartment, some in uniform, some in plainclothes, and some masked. They then proceeded to ransack the place, searching for drugs. They dumped out the boxes in my closet, moved my couch around, and threw my laundry everywhere. The officer who read me my rights told me that I was under suspicion for drugs, and that they had a warrant. I stood there in shock, barely able to process what was going on around me.

A lot of things went through my head that night, while my face was pressed firmly against my living room wall. My life was done, and I was going to jail. My hopes and dreams were dashed. My job was gone. I thought about how my mom would react, how disappointed she would be. And I realized that this was what I deserved. I had countless warnings, countless opportunities to change, and I didn't. I was an idiot, and maybe there wasn't any other way. I knew I would quit if I was in jail. I thought back to my car problems the day I had gone to buy the bag these cops were here to get. I did find it weird that they had brought such a large team for such a small bust. It just didn't make sense.

I began to try to analyze the situation in a little more depth. The first thing I thought was that someone had smelled the weed I was smoking earlier and called the cops. *They sure brought the whole house for a simple suspicion of smoking pot,* I thought. But that didn't make sense, because I always smelled neighboring apartments' weed in the hall. I thought maybe the cops had been watching me since I got off probation; but still, I hadn't been having a lot of visitors or engaging in any suspicious behavior. That couldn't be right. I thought maybe they were trying to bust me on some old case, for some drugs I may have sold years ago, but then why were they searching for new evidence? It couldn't be that. It even crossed my mind that they might have been trying to set me up, and that they were going to come out of the bedroom with something that wasn't even mine. Then I thought of something that *was* mine. Where did I put that bag, after I had smoked out of it just hours ago?

My mind scrambled, but I couldn't remember where I had hidden it. My typical hiding spots were pretty obvious, and I usually just shoved it under the couch. Apparently I didn't put it there, because they had already looked. I couldn't for the life of me remember where I had put it.

The search was wrapping up and my apartment was trashed. I could tell they had found something, as two of the cops were standing in the kitchen holding some small item and talking. A uniformed officer took me in my bathroom and began to play the twenty-questions game I had become familiar with just eleven months earlier. I answered them all, and was taken to the kitchen.

"So what do you have to say about this?" said one of the cops, pointing to the counter.

I looked down and saw some of my rolling papers sitting there. Confused, I shrugged my shoulders.

A high-ranking officer in street clothes uncuffed me and took me in the bedroom. I still wasn't sure what to expect, or if I could get in trouble over rolling papers. I wondered what had happened to my bag.

"I know you smoke pot," he started, "I can still smell it in here. We have a warrant to search your apartment, but we were looking for three men who do not match your description."

"So you searched my apartment in error?" I asked, confused.

He didn't answer, but continued. "We found rolling papers here, which are indicative of the fact that you do indeed smoke marijuana, but we could find no further evidence. But I will offer you one bit of advice. Quit smoking pot! We'll overlook the rolling papers this time."

He handed me a warrant that did indeed have my address on it. With that gesture, over an hour after they had burst through my door, the entire raid team left my apartment. I stood there stunned.

I sat down for a minute in a daze, just reflecting. What were the odds of that happening, especially at such a critical point in my life? A police raid, to the wrong apartment, on the day I had called in sick, a few weeks after I bought my first bag after probation? In my wondering, I happened to glance down at the carpet, and there I saw the roach I had put on my lamp stand. In their rampage, the cops must have knocked it on the floor. I again began to wonder where my bag could have been hidden. I looked under the couch, and it wasn't there; it couldn't have been or they would have seen it. It wasn't on the lamp stand shelves, and it wasn't under any rubble in the living room area. I went in the kitchen, and opened the drawer. There sat a box of Philly Blunt cigars, and inside was my pot, untouched. I couldn't believe the cops didn't find it.

I was at a decision point in my life. I had two options: continue along the party path I had known for over five years, or enter the uncharted terrain of a Christian lifestyle. I was finally gaining an understanding of just how critical that decision was, and that it had to be made before it was too late. And the way I was going, the next day could have been too late.

date: december 1, 2004
purpose: follow-up to takeover meeting
agenda: the new program

Alcohol stood at the door of the boardroom, giving each of the members an evil fake smile and greeting as they entered. There was a deathly depressing air as the Committee slowly reconvened. Lust and Pot sat on either side of the chairman's spot, and the rest of the members timidly claimed their seats around the table. After all of the members, excluding Life, were in the room, Alcohol shut the door and walked proudly to the chairman's seat and sat down.

"Welcome, welcome, everybody," he began, with a haughty tone. "Welcome to the new era of the Committee. I am Chairman Alcohol, and you know my associates." He gestured to either side of him. "Now we have many things to discuss, so let's get right down to business. First off, Finance, we are absolutely done with contributing to the church, thank you."

"But I don't really..." started Finance.

"Oh, see, you don't really get it, Finance," interrupted Alcohol. "These topics aren't debatable anymore. They're just how it's going to be from here on out. Please, I encourage you *not* to contribute, for your own sake, or you'll end up gone, like your good buddy Life. No more money to the church. What else is on the list, Pot?"

Pot looked down at the clipboard in his hands. "Um, Society," he said.

"Yes, Society," said Alcohol. "No more church for you. You'll have to get reacquainted with your party buddies, 'cause they're the only people you're going to be seeing. None of these clueless goodie-two-shoes for you. Next?"

"Health," said Pot.

"Health, I'd love to keep you around," said Alcohol, "but unfortunately, that takes a lot of work. Workouts and sports are times that could be spent getting drunk or high, and that's kind of what we're leaning toward with this program," he said, feigning concern. "And the foods you like, they taste like crap, so they're out. Competition, you're going to have to find an outlet different than sports. We will, however, accept video games. Next?"

"Conscience," said Pot.

"Conscience, you're just going to have to shut up," said Alcohol. "That's all we want out of you. Shut up, or join Life."

Suddenly, there was a gentle knocking at the board-room door.

"What's that?" asked Happiness.

"Pay no attention to that," commanded Chairman Alcohol. "It's nothing, I assure you. Happiness, glad you spoke up. We have no place for you here, buddy. You can also keep your mouth permanently shut like Conscience, or be booted. Who's next on the list, Pot?"

"Logic and Pleasure," replied Pot.

"Logic and Pleasure," repeated Alcohol. "My two favorites. Logic, you may continue on the same path you've been on, gathering information and making 'brilliant' conclusions. No more God research though, please. Spend your time a little more wisely. And help us maintain our course."

"But I don't like 'our course'," objected Logic. "'Our course' doesn't seem so logical any more."

"Don't throw away a chance to reign with us," said Alcohol. "I assure you, other courses I can choose would be worse. What, you're going to start actually believing in God? And Pleasure, you get exactly what you wanted. Almost everything we do is for your betterment. You get to live that party life you wanted, and you get to live it to the fullest. In fact, you get to party until you die."

"That has never been what I wanted," said Pleasure regretfully.

"Anyone else on that list?" asked Alcohol.

The knock at the door came again, this time a little louder.

Pot looked up and then back to his clipboard. "Greater Good," he read.

"The newbie, huh?" asked Alcohol. "Greater Good, you are even more useless to this new Committee than Happiness. Why should we give any concern about others, in or outside of this Committee?"

"Because this Committee's well-being hinges on others, not just itself," replied Greater Good, more defiantly than the other members. "And you and your minions do not belong on this Committee!"

The knock came a third time, louder still.

"You're getting a little too bold for your own good..." said Chairman Alcohol to Greater Good.

"You've always been too bold for your own good," Greater Good quickly returned.

"You're finished, old man!" said Alcohol standing quickly to his feet. "Give me a hand," he said to Pot. They angrily moved toward Greater Good and grabbed his arms.

The fourth knock at the door was loud and aggressive. Happiness couldn't sit still any longer. He jumped to his feet, ran to the door, put his hand on the knob, and looked up with a grin.

"Don't do it!" threatened Alcohol, "or you're gone too."

Happiness flung the boardroom door wide open. Life stood behind it with a confident smile on his face that eclipsed his many cuts and bruises. He walked in, eyes intent on Alcohol, and gently closed the door.

"Life, we beat you down once, and we can do it again," said Alcohol angrily, throwing Greater Good to the floor.

"Not this time," said Life calmly. "This time, *we* are eliminating *you*."

"You don't have the strength to stand against us!" mocked Alcohol.

"We have been building that strength since the Christmas that Conscience spoke up," said Life confidently. "Who will stand with me?" he asked the other members.

"I will stand with you," said Happiness, grabbing Life's hand.

"I will stand with you!" exclaimed Conscience, standing to his feet.

"I will stand with you," said Greater Good, standing up from the spot Alcohol and Pot had dropped him. Other members stood to their feet in turn: Finance, Health, Competition, and Society. Pleasure hesitated, but finally stood, fearful of the dark trio's plans.

"How are we going to beat them?" Logic asked urgently from his seat. "They're too strong."

"Leave that to me," said Life. "Please, you have to trust me. You have to trust God's way."

"Don't do it, Baby," Lust said seductively to Logic.

Logic thought for a moment, then stopped. With his eyes locked on Life questioningly, he slowly stood from his seat.

"Oh, it's clean-up time," said Alcohol angrily. "You're all dead. You're dead!" He moved aggressively toward Life, Pot close behind him.

"Stop!" commanded Life.

"Or what?" asked Alcohol, not intimidated and still moving fast.

"Or this," responded Life.

The floor of the boardroom began to rumble.

I awoke to the heavy rapping of the police on the door of my small apartment.

Alcohol and Pot froze. The members looked around in surprise. The floor began to shake violently as all of the members held on to the table.

"Hold on to me, everyone!" said Life. Though the other members were being thrown around by the quaking, Life stood fast, not moving at all. The members quickly gathered around him and held on tight. Alcohol, Pot, and Lust approached the group, a look of terror on each of their faces.

"There's no place for you here!" said Life, with the others huddled around him. The boardroom door flung open, and there was the sound of rushing wind, like a hurricane, creating an immense vacuum in the room. Again, Life seemed to be glued to the ground, but everyone else immediately felt the suction. The chairs started to get tossed around, two of them tumbling out the door. Alcohol and Pot tried to fight the wind, but could not, as both of them flew head-over-heels out the door. Lust held on tightly to the table, and the other members clung to Life. The suction intensified, and Lust was eventually holding on for dear life, as broken chairs whirled about the room. Pleasure was also losing his grip on Life as the strength of the wind grew.

Lust's hands were slipping; she couldn't hold on much longer. She looked arrogantly over at the Committee as one of her hands slipped off.

"I'll be back!" she said defiantly. She lost her grip and flew out the door.

"Help!" cried Pleasure as he too lost his grip. Life quickly grabbed his hand, and the boardroom door slammed shut. The wind and quaking stopped, and the room was again calm.

The door of my small apartment slammed shut behind the raid team as they left with nothing to show for their bust.

A shout of excitement went through the Committee, once again feeling an air of harmony from long ago. Hearty handshakes, and even uncharacteristic hugs, marked the victory celebration. Everyone had a new respect for Life, congratulating and thanking him excessively. He humbly accepted the praise, and encouraged the members to take the triumph to heart.

The members joyously returned to their spots at the table, though most of the chairs had been destroyed. Pleasure and Logic willingly conceded the chairman seat, which was still intact, to Life. After about twenty minutes of excited small-talk, Life called the meeting back to order.

"My friends," he began, "thank you all so much for the part you played in today's amazing success. I am so happy for each of you, and for the Committee as a whole. We are now stronger than ever before."

"It was all you, Life," said Pleasure. "Thank you for not giving up on us. I think that it goes without saying that we will fully adopt the 'God program.' It's time to start making decisions based on what God wants, not just us." A rousing round of supportive applause went through the Committee.

"How did you do that, Life?" asked Logic, still completely baffled. "We thought you were dead! How did you create that stir? How did you draw on something outside of our resources, outside of our control, to eliminate the enemy? How did you..."

"I can explain some of it to you, Logic," began Life, "but beware, it doesn't make logical sense."

"Anymore, what does?" asked Logic, perplexed. "Just tell us, please."

"I petitioned God for a way out of the crushing addiction problems," said Life. "I petitioned him years ago. So he set this all in motion, the crash, the bust, the raid, but he also let us know it was coming."

"How did he let us know?" questioned Logic.

"Well, how many warnings did we get over the years?" asked Life. "We were on the wrong track, but we could get glimpses of the right one, mainly as we began to understand Greater Good. Greater Good is how God works; he set this planet up to operate yielding the best possible outcome for the people he has selected. Seeking after God began to give us a general understanding of his plan, the Greater Good."

"So who has he selected?" asked Logic.

"No human knows about anyone else, or can decide for anyone else," answered Life. "The only person we have any control over is ourselves. And God selects us if we select him."

"So we selected God by making a unanimous decision to follow his ways?" asked Logic.

"It's a little more complicated than that," said Life. "We have been making this decision for our entire life, and we need to continue making it. We had a lot of negative built up, and had to counteract it with a lot of positive. The transition was slow, but we eventually chose his ways wholeheartedly, defeating our oppressors. Choosing God started with the decision we made years ago, almost subconsciously, to accept his plan. That choice has blossomed into tonight's impressive victory, not to mention the victories to follow."

"That doesn't really make much sense..." said Logic.

"I warned you it wouldn't," said Life. "But I also told you that faith is a required element of this connection. When you exercise a little faith, the answers become more apparent even to the logical parts of the mind. Greater Good has some of these answers."

"Why are you helping us after all the resistance we put up against you?" asked Logic.

"Well, since God gave life, he also figured he should set up a way to be successful at it," answered Life. "Every human gets a dose of life and true happiness as a child. Every human can neglect these gifts, or can cultivate them starting with the help of two of God's tangible resources—the Bible and the church. So we started to cultivate them, and God gave us that extra push we needed to succeed."

"Interesting..." replied Logic.

"Choosing God signs us up for a lifetime of 'technical support' in the form of me, Life... the connection to him. And through this connection, you are allowed many benefits. Once we get on his program, his goal and promise is that all things work together for the good of his followers collectively and individually."

"That's kind of a hard pill to swallow," said Logic.

"Well, haven't the events of the past four years resulted in the victory over the forces that were oppressing us? Each element played its role: the realization, the crash, the move, the brownies, the raid. Some seemed bad, and some good, but the overall conclusion has to be that each of these events played its necessary part in the beauty of victory."

"That is the truth, I suppose," agreed Logic.

"I'm not asking you to go from atheist to priest over-night, Logic," said Life. I'm just asking that you move slowly away from the doubt, and begin to build your faith. I will show you everything that you need to know from there."

"I guess I'm going to have to, after what happened tonight, and over the last four years," answered Logic. "So you've been planning this 'takeover' for a while?"

"Sort of," replied Life. "You have always had the abil-ity to choose, and each member chose my plan for a dif-ferent reason. Conscience was the first to remember what the parents said about drinking and drugs, and about God. From there, a sorrowful Happiness remembered how God had been a big part of his joy. Competition is an easy sell on a challenge like quitting or living mor-ally. Finance made a big gesture of faith, partially out of protest, based on the crash. Health also wanted change as fitness decreased continually. Many of these members *had* to be pushed to the edge, to see how bad life could get for them before they would change their mind. Like Pleasure, and you, Logic. That's why God allowed the Greater Good into our lives—to shake us up and push us to the point where we would each choose God. A unani-mous decision alone in the human mind might not be enough to win over all of our enemies, but a unanimous decision *with* the power of God is enough to overcome anything this world throws at us. And this is why we over-came; because the power of God is with us."

"But how?" asked Logic, perplexed. "Who are you, really?"

"I am your personal link to God," said Life. "I bridge the gap between God and man. I am the Life every person clings to so tightly. I am the Truth about existence. I am the Way into God's plan and heaven. I have always been a part of you. I have always been with you. I have always been your gift of life. All you have to do is follow me. I am Jesus."

chapter 14: **decision time**

thought this life was all about me. It wasn't. I thought my story was about my addictions, but it wasn't. I thought it was all about *my* strength, and *my* resolve, and *my* wisdom, but as it turns out, my minuscule contributions had very little to do with my life's outcome. I realized as I sat in my apartment that the choice I made at birth, the choice to live, had to be made many times in life. I also realized where that choice had come from. It didn't come from me, or anything I had done. It came from God.

I thought back to a prayer I had made as a child. I could barely remember it, but my mom had filled me in on the details. She said it was "so precious" how I had prayed so sincerely while rolling around on the couch with my eyes tightly shut, talking to God. It didn't bother God that my attention span was so short, or that I was only five. He willingly accepted me into his family. At age five, I had made a choice that changed my life forever.

In later years, God became an elusive concept to me. I had a lot of trouble finding him, but I really wasn't looking as I began my descent into drugs and alcohol. Finally, when I realized something was wrong, I decided to do some research into God. I began to seek him, as I failed monumentally in solving my own problems. As I sought more, I found more. And as I understood God's plan, piece by piece, I realized that he had been looking for me all along. In fact, he had been a part of me throughout my search.

God had given me a built-in link to him, in the form of his son, Jesus. Recognizing and accepting this connection fulfilled me at the deepest level, though my depression required additional work. But God didn't leave me with just some abstract feeling. He gave me the Bible and other literary sources of encouragement. He gave me a church as a social resource. He gave me a challenge: living for him. He gave me the ability to talk to him, understand him, through my link, Jesus. Though it hadn't seemed like he was listening in the past, I realized that all along he had been doing better than just listening. He had been setting me up for success. It was time for me to take the final step, and *choose* that success.

Sitting alone in my apartment, I finally knew that I wasn't really alone at all. I prayed for a moment, and reflected for a moment. I didn't know how many more warnings God was going to send my way before it was too late and I destroyed myself. I decided that I had better take this one to heart. The "odds" of this particular sequence of events—the crash, the New Year's bust, the probation, the drug tests, the new job, the raid—seemed to be one in a trillion. How could it ever work out like that? But the fact that such a course was so unlikely made me feel very special. God had set all of that up for me. It was about time I did something for him.

So I did it. I sold out to the moderately "crazy" Christian lifestyle. I suppose some people thought it was a loss for the "logical side," but I couldn't let that matter to me. I had given every aspect of my life a chance to change—a chance to provide me with the happiness I lacked. Everything had a chance to make me happy. Only one thing worked: the pursuit of God. With all the arguments against him, I needed only to fall back on one thing. In December of 2001, I wasn't happy. In December of 2004, I finally was.

I took the remainder of my bag and my roach into the bathroom and flushed them down the toilet. With 2005 just around the corner, I made the resolution to quit drinking and smoking pot and cigarettes. But I knew I had to do more than just make a commitment; millions of people did that every year. I had to *live* that commitment. My past was written, but the pen was still in my hand, and many blank pages spanned before me. And although I was the one holding the pen, the Author was the one who inspired the story.

As 2005 began, I signed up for a class at my church and began to get as involved as I possibly could. Every Sunday, Monday, and Wednesday, I was there, not because I loved to be preached at, but because I needed the help of God and his family to succeed. I finally realized that success was not going to happen in my life without following God and his plan. It was the simple "cause and effect" principle. Choosing God caused success. Not choosing God resulted in failure.

In 2005, with God's help, I succeeded in defeating my addictions. I continued to search out God and become more familiar with his ways through prayer, Bible reading, and church. And though the connection has always been difficult for me to understand, my continuing commitment to God's plan has yielded both emotional and physical blessings in my life. Those blessing continue to this day.

Today, I lead an "average" life. There's really nothing special about my story, my background, or my appearance. *Having God in my life is what makes me special.* God's path has already elevated me beyond what I thought I could accomplish. I thought I would be drinking and drugging forever. I haven't touched any of it—drugs, alcohol, or tobacco—since 2004. I thought I would be confined to mediocrity in my career. Since I've been seeking God, I have been promoted repeatedly, most recently to a position in which I get to travel the country. I thought I had spoiled my chances of finding a quality girlfriend with my past exploits. Now I have a beautiful supportive wife, better in every way than I could have imagined. I thought I would never be happy again. Today, I am.

profile: greater good

The Committee faced some important restructuring issues as a result of Life's victory. Life became the undisputed chairman, with Greater Good as his right-hand-man. Logic retained some authority, and most of the other members received some promotion. More time was spent in the gym and playing basketball. A better grasp was gained on finances. Conscience spoke, and the others listened. Happiness was revitalized. Society was re-educated. The only member who took a major hit in status was Pleasure.

Pleasure didn't like his new position, but he had to realize that it was for the best. If he had continued his rule, the result would have been death, and then no one would get any enjoyment. He still fought for his viewpoints, but the other members kept him in check. Sometimes he was even shunned. And although he often didn't get along with the "God program," he had to admit it was for the best. For this reason, Greater Good still looked out for him. As long as Pleasure wasn't lived for, he could continue on the Committee.

With the new structure in place, a new era began. The new era would be marked with success and joy—mere concept under the previous regime. Greater Good, God's plan, slowly brought new viewpoints to light as the Committee recognized his authority. God wasn't a pleasurable or social choice. He didn't even seem logical much of the time. But anytime God didn't seem visible, Greater Good encouraged the Committee to take a step back. He encouraged them to look at the bigger picture. And sure enough, every time the proper vantage point was taken, there was God, working behind the scenes. There was Jesus, encouraging me to follow him.

I had seen enough despair in my life. So I accepted God's plan for me. And I finally realized that this was the objective of life. This was the goal of the whole sequence of life-events. This is what the Committee had ultimately been deliberating from the start. We are given one life-time, some longer than others, to determine the answer to one very simple but complex question: "Will you follow God?" My unanimous answer is *yes*.

About **the Author**

Clay Cornelius lives in Lansing, Michigan with his wife Danielle and their big yellow lab. Clay travels the United States, mainly the East Coast, as part of his job as an auditor. He and his wife are members of Mount Hope Church, and Clay frequently helps with the juvenile ministry. He is also taking classes at the church to continue to build his understanding of God's plan for his life. He enjoys playing basketball and working out. It is Clay's hope that this book will help others understand that help is only a prayer away. A committed relationship with the Lord is enough to overcome any problem, great or small.

Clay would like to hear from you. If you enjoyed his book, or hated it, please mail him directly at:

Clay Cornelius
P.O. Box 80106
Lansing, MI 48908

Or e-mail him at:
tc-cornelius@comcast.net

He would love to hear your comments, questions, and criticisms. Please write!